To Emma
You're a
"apple of gold"... Keep
shining with THE RIGHT
TALK!

RIGHT TALK

Blessings
Iris

An Inspirational and Practical Guide
to Communications Success

◆◆◆

IRIS FORMEY DAWSON

AN ARTISON PUBLICATION

Published by Artison Publications
P.O. Box 13314
Savannah, Georgia 31416

Cover concept & design: Stephen Owiro

All Biblical Scripture referenced herein has been cited from the New King James Version.

PRINTED IN THE UNITED STATES OF AMERICA

RIGHT TALK

◆◆◆

*An Inspirational and Practical Guide
to Communications Success**

by
Iris Formey Dawson

*Throughout this book, "communication" refers to the exchange of thoughts, messages, or information. "Communications" denotes the art and technique of using words effectively in imparting ideas.

DEDICATION

To my extended family...
those near and dear
and
the dearly departed
(especially my father, Henderson E. Formey, Jr.
and my "adopted dad," George L. Manigault)...
without whose love and devotion
I would not have thrived

CONTENTS

ACKNOWLEDGMENTS

I am especially grateful to...

My husband and children—Arthur, Eric and Nia
for being "the wind beneath my wings"

My parents—Henderson E. and Eloise C. Formey
for making and molding my wings expressly for top flight

My brothers and sisters—Sylvester, Gregory, Donald & Creswell
Formey, Jennie Hall, Wilhemenia Buckner (my editor) and Andrea
Williams & their families
*for always "believing I could fly," "sponsoring my trips" &
"cushioning my landings"*

My grandmother, Leola Lundy and my aunts, Erma Stripling &
Betty Jean Williams
for keeping the ancestral fires burning

My mother-in-law, Charlotte Dawson, and sisters-in-law, Gwendolyn
Greene, Lazette Michael, Gilda Goings, and Effie Ellis
& their families
for bridging the gap with family love & support

My adopted "mom," Charlene Manigault (& "siblings": Wendell,
Donna, Marcia, Terry & Renelly); my "right-hand sisters": Vera
Robbins, Peggy Bolden, Ellaree Peters & Pat "Gail" Green
for being a "second family" par excellence

My cousins, Danny and Paulette Patterson; Carolyn Coleman;
Cheryll Davis; and Carmen Jones & nephew, Dennis Greene
for sparking amazing high-tech and human connections

My pastor, Dr. Ricky Temple & his wife, Diane
*for extraordinary support & inspiring me to take flight under the
strength of my own wings to finish this project*

My mentors, Aberjhani; Vera J. Hilliard & Charles McMillan
for showing me how to maximize my wingspan

The Savannah Tech Library staff—Jim Burch, Jeanese Riley & Suk Bradt
  for continuing unparalleled research and presentation support

My "brother," Leroy Bolden; Iesha Brown; Stephen Owiro & Angela Washington-Blount
  for technical assistance "extraordinaire"

Bruce Habersham, Alfredo Alponte, Julian Santa-rita, Brandon Royal, Bernadette Ball-Oliver & Judi Palmer
  for helping me develop a first-rate promotional tool while I was completing this book

Larry Chisolm & the King-Tisdell Cottage Foundation
  for inspiring and facilitating the first public TALK RIGHT workshops

Janet Cuttray, Gwendolyn German, Angela Smith, Gail Terrell & Aimee Thompson
  for always being there for Nia and me

Helen Braddy and Emily Quarterman
  for being there when & how Daddy, M'dear & the rest of us needed support the most

Byrdell Bryant, Doris Cooley, Grace Cuyler, Evelyn Baker Dandy, Ellen Flood, Alfred & Zoe Fountain, Freddie & Alfreda Goldwire, Mary Jackson, Avais Jones, Bobbie & Leila Jones, Sharon Lemon, Altheria & Carmelita Maynard, Huxsie Scott, Catherine & Laurita Taylor, Karen Taylor-Collins, Andy & Margie Williams
  for "feeding me" encouraging, informational and healthy tidbits throughout the years

All my other family and friends who've supported me and my work throughout the years
  for helping to keep my spirit and body going

PREFACE

I was blessed with the most remarkable parents! While successfully rearing seven children on a public educator's salary and a homemaker's ingenuity could *not* have been easy, Daddy and M'dear always made it seem so. Undergirded by an abiding faith in God and confidence in themselves as a team, Henderson E. and Eloise C. Formey implanted within our spirits and souls the best that each of them had to offer. They filled our "everyday world" with the brilliant sunshine of the RIGHT TALK—verbally and nonverbally—and because of that gift, we all have flourished!

Through both word and deed, these Baxley, Georgia natives powerfully inspired not only their household and our neighborhood to place a premium on self-improvement—but thousands of others as well. Daddy, though average in physical stature, was *an oratorical giant.* His mastery of the written and spoken word catapulted him to the helm of the Savannah-Chatham County (Georgia) Public School System, earning him the distinction of being the first African American to hold the position. Likewise, in his service to the Lord as a Christian minister and pastor, he moved many a congregation with sermons that rightly divided the Word in one of the most fluid styles ever to have graced this earth. In both capacities, he bore the fruits of "right" thinking.

Publicly, much more verbally reserved than my father, M'dear has always been no less of *a masterful mover and shaker.* Through many personal trials and family challenges, her brilliance has shone in her regal poise and wisdom. As the unquestionable navigator of our family, consistently, her impeccable attention to detail and "doing things right" has spoken volumes about her steadfast spirit of excellence. A *magna cum laude* clothing and textiles major, she continues to model for us (and all who meet her) the winning ca-

xi

pacity of a polished physical presence.

Thus, as if by genetic *and* environmental design, I have fashioned this book after the complementary gifts of my parents—two priceless, shining *apples of gold.* Guided by the light of their legacy, may you embrace the fuller, "fitter" life ahead as you fill your world with the RIGHT TALK—verbally and nonverbally!

IRIS FORMEY DAWSON

NOTE: This guide was developed as a practical, inspirational refresher to boost your present level of communications fitness. My desire is that you use **RIGHT TALK** as a starter tool to refocus and sharpen your commitment to build more effective communication skills. In that light, it should not be viewed as a substitute for personal coaching or enrollment in comprehensive language, speech, or image-building courses. I purposely chose not to write this book on a "scholarly" level but rather to take a distinctly lighter approach to highlight solutions to some of the most common communications challenges. So...kick off your shoes, roll up your sleeves, and dive right in!

> "Hold yourself responsible for a higher standard
> than anybody expects of you. Never excuse yourself."
> — Henry Ward Beecher

Chapter 1

THE GOOD, THE BAD & THE UGLY
Language from Three Perspectives

Language has standards of excellence against which anyone's performance can be measured. Even so, depending upon the circle you are in, you may think that language is *all* good, *some* bad, or that it really doesn't make a difference how anyone speaks. Too many people say, "Communication is communication. As long as you get your point across, why should it really matter *how* you sound?"

Well...they have a point. *If* they don't care about making good impressions...*if* they intend to live in a vacuum and talk only to themselves...*if* they have no desire to rise any higher than where they are right now.

Most sane people, however, do not relish the thought of living the static life of a hermit. We realize that excellent communication skills *do* make a difference. Especially in a society in which technology just about takes care of everything else, your facility of speech, your know-how, can make or break your image. *Poor* language skills can be the bane of your existence (an albatross around your neck—dragging you down to miserable depths). *Adequate* language skills can be a pretty good equalizer. They can put you on level footing with many others, winning you much-deserved respect. *Excellent, truly outstanding* language skills, however, can be the "wind beneath your wings"—lifting you to heights you have only imagined.

LAYING DOWN THE STANDARD

One sure way to soar above the crowd (and to remain so) is to live "the good life" of a Master Communicator. Communication is the hinge upon which many doors of opportunity open and close.

Understanding this truth is essential to success. Often, it's a major reason that some people fly high and others just can't seem to get off the ground—personally *and* professionally. This is not to say that *everyone* at *all* times should be expected to speak perfectly. Because that's unrealistic. In fact, most people (even many of the best communicators) use a blend of formal and informal, standard and nonstandard speech. Why does this blending work better for some people than it does for others? Again, know-how is the principal difference.

When you clearly establish that you *can* speak well, you can "afford" to relax your language a bit. Many speakers do this purposely to try to make a stronger connection with the general public or a particular group, such as teenagers. And some people are simply bidialectal. That is, they naturally (and quite consciously) slide between standard and nonstandard speech. While this is known as "pivoting" in speech pathology circles, I call it "dimmer-switching." People who *decide* to use two distinctly different speech patterns—usually one publicly and another privately—control their tongues like a dimmer modulates a light. They purposely adjust the intensity, or sharpness, to best serve their intentions in a given setting to fit the occasion, activity or mood.

For too many others, however, this is not the case. Their use of nonstandard English is often unintentional. Therefore, since they don't know enough about standard speech, they should strive to speak their best both in and out of the public eye—or *ear*. As with anything else, consistent private practice is the only way to sharpen public performance. It's one of the keys to opening the door to greater fulfillment and opportunity.

ADDRESSING THE TRUTH OPENS DOORS

In American society, certainly, it is no secret that many people suffer the injustices of a number of "isms," such as racism, sexism, and classism. In other words, they are discriminated against due to no fault of their own. Consequently, it is understandable when complaints of wrongdoing are lodged. In fact, in such unquestionable cases of mistreatment, outcries for justice are reasonably expected.

On the other hand, there are individuals who behave badly and cry wolf when no wolf, in fact, is anywhere on the prowl. Instead, they find it convenient and more comfortable to whip up hysteria and try to divert attention from themselves. They project their shortcomings onto someone else, attributing them to some reason that lies beyond the realm of personal responsibility. These artful dodgers seem pre-programmed to blame anyone and anything other than themselves. Thus, they float around in mock denial and find it rather easy to conjure up ideas of being under siege. Their trademark knee-jerk reaction allows them to insulate, or shield, themselves. It "protects" them from a true reality check. It keeps them from fully facing the notion that some of the rejection they experience is the product not of injustice, but of personal inadequacy instead.

BEING IGNORANT IS *NOT* BLISS

An even sadder reality is that, in too many other cases, accusations of discrimination fly because the alleged victims *simply don't know any better*. They are very much unaware of the fact that the "culprit" is within. They haven't realized that they are sleeping with, walking with, and talking with the real enemy—their *own* tongue, demeanor, or physical image. They don't know that they have literally "talked" themselves *out of* more opportunities than anyone else could have or even wanted to deny them. Because of poor verbal and nonverbal skills, they have been relegated to the fringes of mainstream action. You might say they have had to pay a high price to watch a game they are not allowed to play.

Even more of a tragedy is when someone *behaves badly* after (unbeknownst to them) being rejected as a result of poor speech and the limitations it brings. Some people act up, show out, and even get downright ugly when things don't go their way. Their inclination is to get huffy and point the finger at someone else. Determined not to curl up in a corner, lick their wounded egos, and sulk, instead, they explode into an unbelievable tirade. Ranting and raving and...continuing to butcher the English language. Of course, such a very unattractive display only confirms any decision to pass over or shut out the clueless protester. But, unfortunately, in instances like this, seldom does any thought of personal responsibility enter into the picture. And if it ever does, speech deficiencies are *not* part of the equation.

ACCEPTING AND WORKING WITH THE TRUTH IS *GOOD*

In the communications arena, it's reassuring to know that in the midst of both "The Bad" and "The Ugly," there is still a great deal of good. There are good attitudes of good people who appreciate that sometimes there may be things they need to work on. Many of them readily acknowledge that there are areas they can improve. They accept that their language problems could erect barriers to advancement. And these good people make up their minds to do whatever it takes to turn their situations around—to go around, leap over or run right through such barriers to success.

Those who are most successful take well-calculated routes to their destinations. Before striking out to change their destinies, they equip themselves with an excellent plan of action and a steel will. That is, knowing that following a plan is not always easy, they strengthen their chances of a positive outcome by maintaining an unbreakable will. And the two combined are usually unstoppable.

TAKE INVENTORY

What are some basic ingredients of a great communication skills building plan? Like most great plans for change, a wise place to start is with a written inventory. (Use the one on pages 7 & 8 to assess both your verbal and nonverbal skills.) First, to be sure you get a good reflection of your strengths and weaknesses, do a self-assessment. Just remember that when taking stock of what you do and don't do well, it is extremely important to be honest with yourself.

Then, ask someone (whom you can trust *to tell you the truth*) to point out positives and negatives she has observed in you. In fact, to see if a gap exists between your self-evaluation and your critic's perception, have her do an inventory similar to the one you completed. It's very important that this person be someone with excellent communication skills. She must be a competent communicator and committed to your improvement to be able to critique you constructively. So, before reacting badly to the "constructive" criticism of your inventory partner, remember that you *solicited* the input of someone who has your best interest at heart. Prepare to accept your evaluator's opinions and observations graciously. With your blinders off and thin skin out of the way, you should be able to see more clearly where you are as a communicator.

Equipped with a list of communications assets and liabilities, you can begin to work on restructuring your verbal and nonverbal images. You can lay a strong foundation for building on your strengths and minimizing your weaknesses.

BROADEN YOUR HORIZONS

Once your foundation is firmly in place, concentrate on broadening your horizons. Proceed to erect walls of confidence, vision, knowledge and determination within which you can operate to build a new reality of communications excellence. Then you'll experience greater outcomes.

What you will soon discover, if you maintain a high level of commitment to speaking well, is that your rate of return will *not* equal your investment. Instead, in all likelihood, the rewards will *exceed* your hard work and expectations. When you approach overhauling your speech and physical image with steadfastness, remarkable things are bound to happen. Your bold, new, fresh appearance will attract the very people and situations that have seemed to elude you time after time. Like seed sown in faith and tended with utmost care, your time and dedication to enhancing your skills have the capacity to yield spectacular results!

STAY OPTIMISTIC

The positive energy you send out will bring the same to you. Experts have found that this is an immutable law of the universe. That is, it is a fact of life that does not change. When you exude goodness and excellence—goodness and excellence (for the most part) find and embrace you.

Sure, there will be naysayers who criticize your upbeat, optimistic attitude towards building a stronger, more excellent system of communicating. But in such instances, you must convincingly say to yourself, "What somebody else's opinion of me is—is *their* business." Properly minding (attending to) your *own* business is certainly enough to occupy you. You have neither the time nor the energy to waste on responding or reacting to anything anybody does in an attempt to tear down your confidence and shake your determination. It is your duty to safeguard the vision you have for yourself. Doing so is critical to advancing you along the pathway to personal improvement.

USE WISDOM AND LET YOUR LIGHT SHINE

To fortify the walls of your commitment to excellent communication, you need to exercise wisdom. Know that *no* amount of knowledge you gain will do you any *lasting* good apart from wisdom (deep, thorough, mature understanding). Wisdom is the internal guide that can direct the flow of your progress. Like a water faucet, wisdom allows you to tap into a remarkable reservoir filled with a life-changing resource that can refresh your life like no other on earth. So, dedicate yourself to the pursuit of wisdom, which is built upon a foundation of excellence.

Do all that you can to improve yourself. Then, once you have increased in brilliance, don't hide your light under a basket. Let it shine and make it your mission to lovingly improve your fellow man, woman, boy and girl. Go into all the world and make a difference! And when you do, you'll truly begin to see the tremendous harvest that is the return of the seed you sowed so long before. Surely, the blessings of God will overtake you. As the biblical Scripture Luke 6:38 states, "Give, and it will be given to you: good measure, pressed down, shaken together, and running over will be put into your bosom. For with the same measure that you use, it will be measured back to you." Simply put, embrace and share The Good, and your life will have no more room for either The Bad *or* The Ugly.

COMMUNICATIONS SKILLS INVENTORY

Record your first response to each of the following statements:

(1) As a communicator, I _____

_____

(2) As a communicator, I do not_____

_____

(3) To get my points across, I _____

_____

For each statement below, circle the response that describes you:

I listen to others attentively, without interrupting.	ALWAYS	SOMETIMES	RARELY
I maintain eye contact respectfully.	ALWAYS	SOMETIMES	RARELY
My gestures appropriately complement my speech.	ALWAYS	SOMETIMES	RARELY
I get my points across clearly and succinctly.	ALWAYS	SOMETIMES	RARELY
I pronounce words well.	ALWAYS	SOMETIMES	RARELY
I drop or understress certain word sounds.	ALWAYS	SOMETIMES	RARELY
I walk into a room with confidence.	ALWAYS	SOMETIMES	RARELY
I speak with energy and passion.	ALWAYS	SOMETIMES	RARELY
I operate well in business social settings.	ALWAYS	SOMETIMES	RARELY
I use standard English well in business settings.	ALWAYS	SOMETIMES	RARELY
I dress appropriately for my profession.	ALWAYS	SOMETIMES	RARELY
My speech reflects a broad vocabulary.	ALWAYS	SOMETIMES	RARELY
I stammer and pause when I speak.	ALWAYS	SOMETIMES	RARELY
I maintain excellent grooming & hygiene.	ALWAYS	SOMETIMES	RARELY
I speak in a monotone.	ALWAYS	SOMETIMES	RARELY
I adjust my volume to fit various occasions & settings.	ALWAYS	SOMETIMES	RARELY
I speak too fast.	ALWAYS	SOMETIMES	RARELY
I speak too slow.	ALWAYS	SOMETIMES	RARELY
I choose and use words effectively.	ALWAYS	SOMETIMES	RARELY
I struggle to find the right words when I speak.	ALWAYS	SOMETIMES	RARELY
I speak assertively.	ALWAYS	SOMETIMES	RARELY
I speak aggressively.	ALWAYS	SOMETIMES	RARELY
My posture is good.	ALWAYS	SOMETIMES	RARELY
I use originality in my oral presentations.	ALWAYS	SOMETIMES	RARELY
My voice is high-pitched.	ALWAYS	SOMETIMES	RARELY

Complete each of the following statements:

(1) What I do particularly well is...

_____

_____

(2) What I don't do well is...

_____

_____

(3) My first focus on improvement should be...

_____

_____

"Without change, something sleeps inside us, and seldom awakens. The sleeper must awaken."
— Frank Herbert

Chapter 2

MUMBLING AND STUMBLING
Speaking Clearly and Powerfully

Many times communication is crippled because people mumble and stumble, hem and haw, jibber and jabber through conversations and presentations. It's as if they have slipped into a quicksand-filled pit and are slowly sinking into a world of muteness, where even if they wanted to cry out loudly and strongly, no longer would there be any hope of getting a message to rise out of the muck and mire.

All too often, individuals with life-changing potential have damaged their chances of making a difference in someone else's life by getting stuck in the mud of the shallow waters of poor communication skills. Generally, people like this, quite overconfidently, believe that as long as the accuracy of the message is on target, the delivery of the message is somewhat incidental. In other words, what's apparently most important to them is having the right stuff to say—rather than *saying the stuff right*.

THE BEAUTY OF THE TONGUE

Have you ever wondered why we are more attracted to some people than we are to others? Even if they don't exactly fit the standard of beauty that American society treasures? Researchers have discovered that, in many instances—regardless of physical image—a person's attractiveness is subconsciously measured by others according to *how articulate he is!* In other words, if you *talk right*, people tend to think that you're "outta sight."

Now, just think about that for a minute. Close your eyes and think of all the "attractive" non-actors you have listened to on television. In particular, let your mind's eye and ear take you back to talk shows where guests' command of the language captured your attention, kept you tuned in, or left you almost breathless. Do you hear them? Do you hear how clear they sound? Do you notice how deliberately their words seem to be chosen, yet how easily they seem to flow off their tongues? Now, do you *see* them? How do they look to you? Poised, elegant, graceful, beautiful, handsome, sexy? You bet!

That's the magic of articulation. It's the wonder of being endowed with the *power* of speech. The word "power" implies a certain forcefulness, an ability to move. And the beauty of it all is that not an ounce of *magic* is involved in it at all. Being articulate (able to speak clearly, distinctly and impressively), while unquestionably a talent implanted in some by God Himself, also can be an art developed by many.

EXAMINE YOURSELF

Have you been *plagued* by mumbling? Do people often seem not to understand fully what you've said? Have you been asked constantly to repeat what you've said, yet you *haven't* been diagnosed with an irreversible speech impediment and you have no reason to believe that your listeners are hard of hearing? If so, don't despair. With some self-examination and self-determination, you can straighten out your situation. Through a simple four-step process, you can go from muffled and ruffled to clear and easy to hear in *no* time.

"Well...I know I don't mumble...but I seem to trip over my lips and get tongue-tied at the drop of a hat...I know what I want to say but it *all* seems to come out in a *jumble*...I don't have trouble actually pronouncing the words...it's just that sometimes I second-guess myself and I'm not quite sure of the words I'm about to use...And by the time I say something, I either *blurt* it out and it sounds *awful* or half of it gets caught in my throat, which is *really* awkward." Sound familiar? If you're such "a stumbler," you're not a lost cause either. Half the battle is acknowledging the problem. The other half is attacking it. By learning and using the steps in this chapter, you can turn your *mumbling* or *stumbling* into a *pace* with *grace*.

Step 1: Check Your Confidence

First of all, you need to do a confidence check. Whether you are painfully shy or overconfident, you can still fall prey to the dastardly duo of Mumbling and Stumbling.

Shyness = Dryness

Let's start with shyness, or the Shell-Less Turtle Syndrome. When turtles need to retreat from potentially threatening things and people, all they have to do is go into their shells, which are handily located. Naturally, by God's grand design, turtles are permanently attached to a relatively strong shelter to which they can withdraw at a moment's notice. Within the confines of their "comfort zone," they feel secure and safe from harm. What an *ideal* arrangement...for a TURTLE!

At last glance, *I* noticed that none of us has joined the reptilian persuasion yet. However, some people retreat so far inside themselves that you'd think they had an actual shell. This tendency is so prevalent that we even refer to such shyness as "being in a shell." Well, if you have been stuck inside an invisible shell, it's time for you to BREAK OUT! By yielding to shyness, you run the risk of missing out on a great deal that life has to offer, *and* you miss out on a great deal of what *you* have to offer life.

In essence, shyness is an offshoot of fear or disgust. When shy people encounter circumstances that frighten or turn them off, and it seems impossible or impractical for them to turn and walk away (when they *really* feel like running), an almost immediate and involuntary reaction is to cower or shrink away on the inside. And this "turtle-like" behavior is simply unacceptable.

You see, you must understand and remind yourself that *God has placed you on this planet to fulfill a distinct purpose.* Each time you deny yourself the opportunity to explore that purpose through interaction with others, you dishonor the gift of self-expression that the Creator has deposited within you. There is no need for you to remain shy—because you were created in God's brilliantly bold image. Therefore, you must *know* and *believe* that, filled with all His greatness, you were *predestined to win!* You were designed to discover and fulfill your purpose on this earth. Therefore, shyness (and the paralyzing fear it often represents) has *no* place in your life.

Whenever the spirit of shyness arises and threatens to sideline and prevent you from engaging in your desires and meeting your obligations, remember your divine nature of greatness. Speak up and out and take advantage of as many opportunities as you can to EXPRESS YOURSELF. Remember that "shyness" equals "dryness." And you don't want to be limited to settling for the dry crumbs off someone else's full plate. You should have an appetite for the finer, more substantive things of life. You should want to sink your teeth into all the richly-textured layers this world has to offer.

Now, if shyness is what shows on the surface, usually low self-esteem is at the root. A shy individual's personality is often bound by feelings of insecurity, fueled by self-doubt. Constantly seeking approval from others, victims of low self-esteem inevitably set themselves up for further spiritual injury because they cling to someone else for personal validation. They tend to relinquish their right of self-approval and invite, even subconsciously, others' opinions to invade their internal worth centers. They just cannot seem to function independently, but rather they live like parasites on a host. Consequently, they expect to derive all they need to survive from an outside source. And that is a dangerous way to live.

People and their opinions can be fickle. Allowing someone else's whims to determine whether or not you thrive is unhealthy. You can't afford to entangle your regard for yourself in a web of esteem for others and their views. Sure, it's fine occasionally to seek the input of others. It's fine to admire them and to aspire to be "like" them. However, your admiration of them must be kept in proper perspective. As far as *your* life goes, their commentary should be secondary. You have to cherish the gift of *your* life. You have to love the blessing of *yourself*.

Quite obviously, there are numerous reasons why people have low self-esteem. One of the most interesting has to do with social programming. Many of us have been programmed to be excessively modest. Though an old saying goes, "Toot your own horn and you'll know it's well tooted," there is a divine directive that says, "Let another man praise you." Many of us have gotten stuck in a state of limbo between these two positions. We're wallflowers stuck at the fringes of life, running the risk of shrinking in the shade of other people's successes. Though we know we possess greatness, we're not so sure that we should step out and be distinguished. We fear that "folks" will label us as arrogant. And we certainly don't want to wear *that* Scarlet "A."

If we stay plugged into our divine connection, however, we would always know how to esteem ourselves in a balanced fashion. I believe that the biblical verse Matthew 5:16 holds the key to breaking this deadlock on the issue of self-esteem. It directs, "Let your light so shine before men, that they may see your good works and glorify your Father in heaven." In view of this admonition, the key is to *embrace* your worth, make your contributions, and let God be glorified as a result. Loving and respecting *yourself* and your part in God's plan honors Him. It also gives you the assurance necessary to speak clearly and boldly and to properly and confidently interact with others.

There is no place for mumbling or stumbling in your life. So, make a conscious decision to CELEBRATE YOURSELF and the blessing of speech. Take the time now to turn to *Study Guide A* (pp. 84-85) and read the sample self-celebratory statements there several times. Afterward, in the space provided at the end of this chapter, write at least one that *uniquely praises YOU*. Practice reading them aloud—speaking as clearly as you can. Then, daily, renew your focus on yourself as the success you declare to be! Make a strategic commitment to monitor and improve your speech patterns. In holding fast to that commitment, you'll discover before long that habitual mumbling and stumbling no longer plague your conversations and presentations.

Beware of Overconfidence

Now, if you're among the ranks of those who have *never had a shy bone in your body*, this "short-and-sweet" segment is for you. Overconfidence can be a speech drawback, too. It can lead to plunging into areas carelessly. It can cause you to speak before thinking, which can amount to communication stumbling. Naturally, you should feel good about yourself and your capabilities. Having a "go-for-it" attitude is terrific—as long as you are adequately prepared. *And* as long as you know your limitations. You see, it is just as important to know your weaknesses as it is to know your strengths. Many times, when people are wading into water too deep for their experience, they flounder around and often stumble when they attempt to discuss issues they are not adequately qualified to speak about. Or, they misuse or mispronounce words.

What makes people give in to the urge to engage in such risky behavior? Again, there are certainly innumerable reasons, but they all seem to be rooted in EGO. Unfortunately, some of us look to outside sources to bolster our self-esteem and every chance we get, we concern ourselves with impressing others. It is this preoccupation with impressions that can push people over the edge and cause them to stumble. The easiest remedy for this problem? JUST BE YOURSELF and BE PREPARED. The next time you are tempted to misspeak, just keep this popular piece of advice in mind: "It is better to be *thought* a fool than to open your mouth and remove all doubt." So, know what you are talking about and use only words with which you are absolutely familiar—especially in public settings.

Another common factor in cases of overconfidence is the "know-it-all" spirit. Some of the major perpetrators of verbal stumbling are *unteachable* people. One of the reasons these types are vulnerable to stumbling is that, by and large, they are not good listeners—to anyone *other than themselves*. Intentionally or unintentionally tuning out others with whom you're having a conversation is an unwise practice. It opens you up to ill-timed statements and responses, which could make for awkward situations.

Keep at the forefront of your mind that learning is a lifelong process. Never forget that we can learn valuable information from the most "unlikely" people during the most "unlikely" times. Be willing to listen and learn before you leap into the depths of any conversation. You may be surprised by what you hear. It might just keep you from what the French refer to as making a "faux pas" and what Americans simply call "falling on your face." Remember, modesty (in moderation) can be a superb safety net.

Step 2: Stay Prepared

The second step in curbing mumbling and stumbling is doing a *thorough knowledge diagnostic*. This particularly applies when you have been asked to speak about a subject with which you *should* be well acquainted. For example, you may be required to do a presentation on a job-related topic or simply asked to respond to a question relevant to your field in general or your position specifically. How prepared you are *long before* even being put in these situations can mean the difference between a letdown and a liftoff.

There are few instances that are more uncomfortable than being forced to put your "ignorance" on public display. Now, don't get offended by the use of the word "ignorant." It has actually taken a beating in our culture. Normally, when we hear it, it has only a negative connotation. However, generally speaking, it merely refers to one's *lack of knowledge*. And there's hardly a quicker way to fall into mumbling and stumbling, stammering and clamoring than to feel that your back is against the wall and you don't know what you should to sound intelligent.

And this doesn't just happen in business settings. Being pressed at everyday social gatherings is no less painful. Therefore, communications wisdom dictates that you PREPARE, PREPARE, PREPARE! Make it your business to learn and retain as much information as possible about your industry, your job, your personal spiritual belief system and current events—including politics. Although for ages it has been believed widely that, in general public conversation, politics and religion are taboo, these days any topic goes. Therefore, no matter the place, the company, or the circumstances, it's best to be as prepared as possible. Before going anyplace where you are likely to have to discuss subjects you may not be well versed in—DO YOUR HOMEWORK! Feeling sure about what you are discussing can cut down considerably on mumbling and stumbling.

Step 3: Step Out Of The Box

Another helpful habit is to steel yourself against extreme reactions to conversation that causes you discomfort. Hardly anything shocks too many people's sensibilities anymore. That is not to say that you have to subject yourself to offensive language or topics. Everyone is entitled to decency according to his own measure. However, there *are* times when your discomfort with conversation has nothing to do with offense. It has instead everything to do with personal insecurity. You may feel out of place in the company of certain people. Especially, you may feel uncomfortable around those whose backgrounds differ from yours.

If this describes you, why not go against the automatic tendency to shy away from those who are different? Why not believe that "variety is *truly* the spice of life" and embrace diversity? Look upon "difference" as something good. Don't view it as controversy waiting to happen. After all, in conversation, opposites *do* seem to attract because there are more questions to be asked and answered. There is more information to share. So, be flexible and venture out by interacting with a wide range of individuals. All in all, your life will be enriched.

You will never know what treasures lie beyond your comfort zone until you step beyond it. Whenever you seek truly to learn about others, you learn a great deal about yourself as well. One fascinating discovery will be that we, *humans*, despite our various walks of life, are more alike than we are different. And that, in itself, should be more than a little incentive for you to walk with both princes *and* paupers, Blacks *and* Whites, Gentiles *and* Jews without ever missing a beat and finding yourself mumbling *or* stumbling.

Step 4: Practice Consistently

I've already mentioned the fourth element in developing a more fluid speech pattern: plain old PRACTICE. Really, its importance cannot be overstated. Once you detect the problems you are having, it is your obligation to yourself to find solutions that fit your needs. Once discovered and adapted to your purposes, practice them *with consistency*. You can never hope to improve your skills substantially and rid yourself of garbled or broken speech if you don't practice with the same fervor that world-class performers apply to their crafts.

Think of a consummate performer—one who consistently outdistances the crowd. It doesn't matter if it's a stellar athlete, an instrumental virtuoso, or a singing sensation. No matter the individual or the field, you know that person didn't reach such admirable heights overnight. What you have come to know as that individual's spectacular, awe-inspiring performances most certainly resulted from long, hard practice filled with adjustment after adjustment.

The challenges that such phenomenons surmount while performing publicly are, in essence, the tip of a very large iceberg. They reflect a mere hint of the beneath-the-surface mass of solid, potentially ship-sinking obstacles that had to be overcome. Superior performers experience success undoubtedly due to unwavering resolve and absolute confidence in their own vision. Such a mindset causes them to *plan to achieve* and to *achieve their plans.* Their performances are so polished because they have endured a great deal of friction to get to the point of shining so brightly. In many instances, despite the odds against them, they have tasted victory time and again because they have refused to see themselves as anything other than winners.

You too can be a repeat winner! You can lessen the probability of continuing to fall short of your communication goals. After examining yourself, assessing your shortcomings, and developing a winning mindset, monitor your speech for stumbles and mumbles. Make the following practical tips central parts of your communication improvement regimen:

1. **Constantly practice enunciating,** or distinctly sounding out, each of your words. To remember common enunciation trouble spots to focus on, refer to the two lists in *Study Guide B* (pp. 88-89).

2. **Sharpen your grammar.** A good place to begin is with the irregular verb tense review in *Study Guide C* (pp. 92-96). Then, consult a grammar refresher text to strengthen other areas.

3. **Choose and use words more effectively.** In business settings, you can reduce and then virtually eliminate inappropriate informal speech, such as slang. *Study Guide D* (pp. 98-99) provides some target examples for elevating your diction (word

choice and usage). Also, the next chapter, *It's Greek & Latin to Me*, discusses the importance of diction in more detail.

Remember, your true communication capacity is a diamond-in-the-rough, waiting for you to use the proper tools to bring it to a glorious luster. You *can* conquer mumbling and stumbling with a realistic plan, persistent practice and unshakable faith.

CELEBRATE YOURSELF

You have greatness within you! So take the time to celebrate YOU. Following the examples in Study Guide A, write at least one brief, catchy statement or poem that reflects your God-given brilliance!

ALLITERATION EXAMPLE

_____

_____

_____

_____

_____

_____

ACROSTIC EXAMPLE *A*

ACROSTIC EXAMPLE *B*

Chapter 3

IT'S GREEK & LATIN TO ME
Vocabulary Building

The value of a broad vocabulary can hardly be questioned. However, for some reason, a wall of mystery stands between too many people and the actual processes of vocabulary building. That wall, however, can be torn down by using a few practical strategies.

The best way for native English speakers to approach vocabulary building is first of all to realize, understand, and BELIEVE that English is English. That is, no matter how unfamiliar and strange an English word may look, it is *not* Greek or Latin or French, Italian, Spanish, Swahili, Chinese or Japanese. In other words, surely if it is your native tongue, you ought to be comfortable with it. Certainly, you shouldn't go around bound by fear that you'll be defeated by a dull, powerless tongue. God gave each of us a tongue so that we could speak gloriously. His intent is that we use it confidently, boldly and well.

APPRECIATE YOUR WORTH

"But you just don't understand; I do pretty well when I stick with what I know. Because I feel more comfortable. In *ordinary* conversation with *ordinary* people, I *ordinarily* do all right." If this sounds all too familiar...*just listen to yourself!* NO ONE is "ordinary!" God's Word says you were *fearfully and wonderfully* made even in your mother's womb! YOU ARE EXTRAORDI-NARY! The word "extraordinary" is fashioned from the Anglo-Saxon or Germanic English prefix "extra-," which means *beyond*, and the Latin root or stem "ord" or "ordinis," which means *order* or *arrangement*. So, if you are extraordinary, that means you were put together from the very beginning in a way that defies or goes beyond "arrangement." And no matter what we do, we can't improve on what God has made. What we *can* do, what we are *expected* to do is honor the substance He has implanted within us and make the most of it.

PERFECT YOUR DIVINE GIFT

In this light, it is our divine duty to seek to perfect whatever God has given us. And since He has given us a tongue (a truly mighty bodily member) we, being created in His image, should hold it in high regard. We should acknowledge that, rightly used, its power is awesome. After all, in Genesis, the very first book of the Bible, we are told that God *"said"*...God *"spoke"*...and the earth and all its fullness came into being, reflecting all of The Creator's splendor.

From a practical standpoint, not developing our "tongue," our *vocabulary,* is much like not sharpening a dull ax and attempting to chop down a tree with it. While our missions may eventually get accomplished, the going will be rough, and the end products might be a bit messy. And since communication can "make or break" an outcome, whether it be a relationship or a business deal, "mess"— we *cannot* afford.

22

Develop a "Bull's Eye" Mentality

We must make excellent communication a target. In archery, the archer's arrow seeks to make a direct hit in the center of the target. In verbal communication, you also seek to use your tongue so skillfully that each time a message leaves your mouth it finds "the bull's eye."

Now, there *clearly* are noteworthy factors that can determine what impact your spoken words make. At or near the very top of the list is diction—your choice and use of words. A prime ingredient in being considered articulate is choosing and using words effectively. It stands to reason that the broader your vocabulary, the more effective you can be in getting your points across and painting images as you wish your hearer to receive them.

The Perception of Intelligence

It is important to elevate your vocabulary because your speech is widely considered to be an indicator or reflection of your intelligence level. Plainly put, people tend to judge you (rightly or wrongly) based on how you speak. I'm sure you've tuned in to a radio or television broadcast or attended a lecture or a sermon and were simply mesmerized by a speaker. Before you knew it, you were caught up by the person's words. Although you may not have been thrilled necessarily by the subject matter itself, you were absolutely amazed by the individual's command of the language.

Chances are some of these people were gifted with the ability to express themselves remarkably. However, in many cases, such eloquence evolved from years of focused effort. Thus, with determination and hard work, you too can significantly develop your communication skills. You can get a firmer grasp of the English language. With a strong vocabulary, you can noticeably heighten your flexibility and improve your image.

WHAT'S IN A WORD?

After wading deeply into a program of vocabulary building, you will discover that a word *is* more than just a word. You will find that the old "a rose by any other name would smell as sweet" approach does not always apply to your speech. It will become more apparent that sometimes using a synonym or substitution phrase *could* make your communication "sweeter." One common argument, or *excuse*, for not using a larger vocabulary is "I thought it was always better to use small words anyway. You know, the shorter, the sweeter...right?"

This is not necessarily true. The question is not the *length* of a word but rather its impression. The number of syllables, alone, does not make a word big or small. Regarding vocabulary, size should be measured relative to familiarity. If a "smaller," or more familiar, word gets the job done, then fine. However, don't underestimate the impact of variety. It can definitely add flavor to your speech.

Not only can a broader vocabulary cosmetically clean up your language, but it can keep you from falling into the pit of redundancy. Unnecessary repetition can bury your message. Have you ever heard people drone on and on using basically the same words over and over again? After a while (in some cases only a very *short* one) you tend to tune them out—often unconsciously. Unfortunately, their weak diction causes their message to be muddled or lost. All because they either didn't take the time or didn't possess the capacity to express themselves well! They didn't bother to consider the listener as they talked.

LET YOUR TONGUE WRITE YOUR TICKET

The power of carefully-chosen and well-spoken words cannot be overemphasized. Enlarging your vocabulary can expand your exposure. Being a powerful communicator can be your ticket into places you thought you'd never have the chance to enter. With a deeper vocabulary not only can you gain entrance into certain business settings, but also you can widen your social circles.

Again, it is simply amazing that people tend to assess your worth based on the weight of your tongue. Surely, you've heard of people who could talk their way *into* or *out of* anyplace or anything. Some individuals *are* gifted communicators. However, if any of them honestly took the time to trace the real evolution of their skill, they would have to agree that constant exposure to excellent communication, along with constant practice, helped them polish their speech.

LISTEN TO ROLE MODELS

If you are really serious about improving your vocabulary, listen to excellent speakers and seek to emulate, or be like, them. "But I'm not around those kinds of communicators on a regular basis. Just about everyone I come in contact with day in and day out talks like I do. So, where am I gonna find a bunch o' folks who speak well and use an impressive vocabulary? What can I do?" Don't fret. That "bunch o' folks" is as close as The Media. That's right. The old "boob tube," *television*, is actually not as bad for our brains as tons of critics would have us believe. You've just got to be selective about what you view and listen to. With cable and satellite TV, there are hundreds, if not thousands, of shows you could find that feature wonderful communicators.

I recommend tuning in to news broadcasts and panel discussions or any such programs where either the language has been scripted *or* conversations have been prepared for. Documentaries are real vocabulary treasure-troves as well. With so many of them airing on networks such as PBS (Public Broadcasting Service), The History Channel, and The Biography Channel, you're bound to find quite a few that interest you. So, record or order videotapes of them for repeated study, focusing on narration and scholarly interviews. Also, don't discount the bonus value of morning news shows. Since their anchors and reporters engage in informal conversations between scripted segments, you can get a good feel for how to comfortably express yourself in business social settings.

You will find communications gems on the radio as well. Many stations air great talk shows and other broadcasts that can be helpful in vocabulary building. Again, choose your "model" shows wisely. Not every radio talk show host or broadcaster speaks well—particularly on the local level. A great place to start is National Public Radio (NPR) or commercial network radio, such as ABC, CBS, CNN, and NBC.

BECOME AN ACTIVE LISTENER

To mine the riches of these shows, you have to be an active listener. That is, engage your inner radar, be on the "listen-out" for unfamiliar or catchy words. Jot them down. If you're unsure about their spellings, try writing a word phonetically, or as it sounds to you. Then, try to find it in a dictionary *or* do the unthinkable—actually venture out into the realm of possible embarrassment and ASK A KNOWLEDGEABLE PERSON FOR HELP.

Who cares what someone else might think of your asking? Remember, what they think of you is nobody's business but their own. What *you* think of your business (your commitment to self-improvement) is exactly that—YOUR BUSINESS. And you have an obligation to tend to it. Forget about possible negative reactions. Stay true to your mission. And get over any bad feelings that you yourself may have about folks knowing there is something you don't know. Remember, there are *no* "all-knowing" people on the planet. God alone is omniscient!

WORK SMART

Learn Definitions

As you know, there's much more to incorporating a "new" word into your vocabulary than simply spelling it right and writing it down. Words often have multiple meanings. And contrary to fantasy—no amount of hocus-pocus or, for that matter, *prayer without hard work* will enable you suddenly to understand fully the meanings of most unfamiliar words. Therefore, you have no choice but to memorize or, at the very least, become very well acquainted with each and EVERY DEFINITION of a new word before you consider yourself qualified to use it—either on paper *or* aloud. And that's just the first step.

Rightfully, you can't claim a word as one of your speech tools (as part of your vocabulary) until you *really* know everything there is to know about it. Without such a depth of knowledge, you can't accurately gauge whether or not you, or anybody else, are using the word correctly. One of the most embarrassing instances you can ever have is when you hear someone use a word in an unfamiliar way and think, self-righteously, *'Uhm, uhm, uhm...they didn't use that word right.'* Then, you go to a dictionary to double-check your "rightness" and discover that *you* were the one at fault. The person simply used a meaning of the word that *you* didn't know.

So, be complete in your quest to learn new words. Keep a vocabulary journal in which you copy each word, along with all of its definitions. Next, practice writing one "different" sentence for every definition of the word. (If you're not sure that you have written them correctly, have an expert check them for you.) Then, privately—alone and with close friends—practice using the word, verbally and in writing, in as many different ways as you can BEFORE "going public" with it.

Master the Pronunciation System

Have you ever heard anybody mispronounce a word so badly that it left you with a sour feeling? Maybe you've even done it yourself—prompting eyebrow-raising, embarrassed glances, or snickering.

Just as millions of people struggle with vocabulary building, they also cringe at the thought of pronouncing certain words. They don't have the slightest idea of how to unravel the "mystery" of pronunciation. Or, equally as bad, they plow through life not really knowing that they say many words incorrectly. In fact, sometimes in mispronouncing a word, they "accidentally" say *another word with a completely different meaning!* Which can totally confuse or mislead listeners given the context of a sentence or a discussion. (For a starter list of words that are frequently confused, see pages 32-33.)

At any rate, pronunciation mastery does not have to be a puzzling, frustrating process. With the aid of a good collegiate dictionary, you *can* decode the "method" to pronunciation "madness." Using the phonetic respelling (located in parentheses immediately after each entry or **bold print** word), you can say any word correctly. Even polysyllabic, or extra long, ones! Or ones with multiple pronunciations.

You may remember from your elementary school years that displayed *at* or *near* the bottom of every (or every other) dictionary page is the pronunciation key—a guide to unlocking the mystery of how to say the respellings. The problem is that many adults have completely forgotten how the key and the respellings work together! (If you're one of those who could use a pronunciation refresher, I have developed the *Sour Notes*™ system—a creative approach that can show you, *in about an hour*, HOW TO PRONOUNCE EVERY WORD IN THE ENGLISH LANGUAGE using a dictionary's pronunciation key. For more details, see page 129).

Learning to use the key and other dictionary symbols properly is actually a pretty simple process. Perfecting it just takes commitment and consistency. And while you're learning, you can check your skill at decoding respellings by using an electronic word pronouncer. That's right...instant audio help with pronunciation is only a handheld or web site away. Most dictionary publishers, including those of the popular Merriam-Webster and American Heritage volumes, not only sell handheld electronic dictionaries but also offer audio pronunciation online.

Particularly in business and social settings, who wouldn't want to be sure about saying words correctly? After all, what good is knowing "what" a word means if you're not sure about "how" a word sounds?

READ...READ...READ

For a more traditional approach to vocabulary building, I dare you to do what so many of us in this vast electronic, fast-paced age won't do much of—READ. In strengthening your vocabulary, reading really *can* be fundamental, like the popular commercial said a number of years ago. If you're really serious about expanding your vocabulary, you'll read and read and READ anything and everything (that you don't find objectionable, of course) that you can get your hands, eyes, and mind on. Just as with the television and radio approaches, be sure to jot down or highlight the words you don't know or are unsure about. Then, look them up and practice using them.

LOOK FOR CLUES

It is not always necessary *or* convenient, however, to interrupt your reading to look up a word's meaning in a dictionary. Instead, you may rely on its context, or surroundings, to help you figure out the meaning. Sometimes, writers *will even give you clues* within the same sentence. Common ones are synonyms (words having the same or nearly the same meaning) and restatements (clearer or different phrasings). Often, information enclosed in commas, dashes, or parentheses also can help you discover what a word means. Try scanning paragraphs before actually reading them for understanding. If you notice pairs of commas, parentheses, or dashes surrounding words or phrases, think of them as caution lights blinking to alert you to look out for the definition or clarifying help sandwiched between them. Just like the information enclosed in parentheses in this paragraph.

Look at the second sentence of the paragraph above. I have used *two* clues that could help a reader pinpoint the meaning of "context"—the synonym *surroundings* and the commas before and after it. Even the single dash in this paragraph signals that additional, explanatory information is coming up.

29

And don't overlook the obvious, a paragraph's general context. You might be able to unlock the meaning of an unfamiliar word merely by paying attention to the message or information in other sentences.

Then there is structural analysis of words—studying their parts to break down meanings. Most American English words have been built from other languages, principally Greek and Latin. Many of them have been developed by taking a basic word form (known as a base, root or stem) and adding a word part to the beginning (prefix) or to the end (suffix). For example, in *disbelieve, dis-* is a prefix. Just familiarizing yourself with prefixes and suffixes (collectively known as affixes) and roots from these languages can boost your ability to *decode* TENS OF THOUSANDS OF WORDS. So, before moving on to the next segment, take the time to turn to *Study Guide E* (pp. 102-111) to begin your study of common Anglo-Saxon, Latin and Greek prefixes, roots, and suffixes.

READING RESOURCES

One especially helpful, readily obtainable vocabulary-building resource is the newspaper. In both national and local papers, read the commentaries and editorials, especially the variety of syndicated columns. These tend to have very rich (flavorful) writing in them because the writers are not bound by the "writing voice" of the newspaper organization itself. Essentially, they are free to express themselves as they wish. Therefore, studying styles and vocabulary choices can be fascinating. Remember, you don't have to agree with a writer's opinions to learn something about language usage. You should approach the pieces objectively—not as a commentator yourself. Read them merely as a student, hungry to learn new words.

Of course, your local library and area bookstores have many books and audiovisual recordings that can help you build your vocabulary. Ultimately, the best advice I can give you is to use every tool at your disposal—people, books, tapes, seminars, TV, radio...THE WORKS!

Whatever avenue you decide to take, just be sure to apply *"the principle of the automobile."* That is, use the gas tank analogy. Developing your vocabulary is like filling a vehicle tank with gasoline. You can go only as far as your gas will take you. Remember, words can fuel progress or stop people cold in their tracks. Just as high-grade gasoline can improve your ride, an excellent vocabulary can positively impact the smoothness of your conversation. You can't expect premium communication experiences if all you've filled your tank with is low-octane words. To stand out, your vocabulary has to be *OUTSTANDING.* Again, that's not to say that you should drive on a tankful of long words. Many of the most powerful "big" words are actually quite short.

The lesson here is don't settle for what's *just good enough* to get your point across. Empower yourself with the richness of the English language. Build your vocabulary strength and truly shine!

WORDS FREQUENTLY CONFUSED

CHALLENGE WORD	OFTEN MISTAKENLY SAID AS
stature (deals with size)	*statue* (as in "monument")
during (deals with time)	*doing* (refers to an action)
brought (past tense of "bring")	*bought* (past tense of "buy")
conscience (deals with moral awareness)	*conscious* (as in "awake" or "alert")
lest (means "for fear that") *has a short "e" sound*	*least* (as in "smallest amount") *has a long "e" sound*
loins (as in hips, groin)	*lions* (as in large cats)
specific (as in definite, particular)	*Pacific* (as in the ocean)
sale (the act of selling) *has a long "a" sound*	*sell* (to offer for sale) *has a short "e" sound*
midst (means "among" or "amid")	*mist* (means "fine drops of liquid")
realm (means "kingdom" or "field")	*rim* (means "edge" or "border")
steel (as in metal) *has a long "e" sound*	*still* (means "free of sound or motion") *has a short "i" sound*

whither (means "to what place")
has a short "i" sound

whether (as in "if")
has a short "e" sound

portion (means "part")

potion (means "a liquid dose")

sure (means "certain")

shore (means "coast")

heresy (as in against a religious belief)

hearsay (means "information heard from another")

accept (means "to receive")

except (means "excluding")

gist (means "central idea")

just (means "fair" or "a moment ago")

burrow (means "to dig or tunnel")

borrow (means "to obtain as a loan")

persecute (means "to oppress or harass")

prosecute (as in legal action)

hail (as in pellets of ice)
has a long "a" sound

hell (as in misery, torment)
has a short "e" sound

partition (means "something that divides")

petition (means "a request to a superior authority")

picture (as in a drawing or photograph)

pitcher (as in a container for liquids)

jewelry (as in accessories)

jury (as in a judging panel)

> "We are what we repeatedly do.
> Excellence, then, is not an act, but a habit."
> — Aristotle

Chapter 4

USE IT OR LOSE IT
Mastering the Art of Telephone Conversation

For many people, one of the most nerve-racking experiences is handling business telephone conversations. In a global marketplace, many transactions are not only initiated by phone but managed almost entirely by remote means.

The first step in developing winning telephone practices is to recognize and appreciate the fact that your voice, coupled with the telephone, has tremendous potential. Together, they can be powerful. That fact, in and of itself, should be a cause for pause because power, as we all know, can be *con*structive or *de*structive. By focusing on positive ways to use your telephone conversations to build your relationships and your business endeavors, you can significantly enhance your value to a company or organization. Or, you can project the value you already know you possess when handling personal business matters. In short, you can accomplish the right objectives.

BE COURTEOUS

Understand that each time you engage in a business conversation, you are asking someone to buy in to something. If you are the caller, your goal is to have the person handling your call take both you and your concern, information, or inquiry seriously. In other words, you don't want to be perceived as a lightweight. Also, as a caller, you cannot afford the baggage that comes with conveying the impression that you are a heavyweight either. No one likes to feel leaned on or intimidated. In the vast majority of cases, what really gives you an effective edge is courtesy.

The key to sounding courteous is starting with and maintaining an air of assertiveness and avoiding aggressiveness at all costs. While blowing steam, breathing fire, and pushing someone around over the phone may make you feel good temporarily, in the long run it can hurt both you and the person on the other end of the line. Remember, although your primary goal may be to get the point across that YOU MATTER, politeness dictates that the other person be made to feel that he matters as well.

RECEIVE CALLS WITH GRACE

The same goes for the reverse situation. When you receive calls, be aware of establishing and maintaining a polite, concerned phone atmosphere—even if the caller is simply seeking mundane, run-of-the-mill, information. Sending the message that the caller counts can make the difference between a positive and a negative phone outcome.

You want the caller to buy the notion that you are interested in the call and that whatever she has to say is important. In fact, how you handle a call can have a ripple effect. It can lay the foundation for future interactions with that person and the many people with whom that individual may come in contact. After all, both good and bad news can travel fast and far. So, don't let poor telephone skills cause ill will to be spread about you or your organization.

ALWAYS BE PROFESSIONAL

The telephone is such an invaluable tool because it enables us to make connections with others in an unmistakably personal way. Certainly, traditional mail, faxes, and e-mail can connect us to others, but nothing can replace the rapport-building power of voice communication. To feel really connected to someone when we can't be there face-to-face, we use the telephone. Even at this stage in our technological advancement, the telephone is the most widely available user-friendly form of communication. Virtually everybody has one and everybody knows how to use it. The question is "Does everyone know how to use it *effectively?*" While many of us may believe that we do—we can always improve.

Whether you are dealing with an in-house or an outside call, you need to be professional with each and every caller. It's not wise to pick and choose the time of day or the persons with whom you feel like sounding professional. Always be prepared to project a business air. It is important to do so no matter how you may feel personally about the person to whom you're speaking.

Also, your feelings about the issues, concerns, or problems being discussed should not cloud your professional performance. You must maintain a respectful personal detachment so that business may be conducted well. This allows both you and the other party to operate on a "win-win" level, where both of you leave the conversation feeling satisfied that courtesy was extended and maintained.

MONITOR YOUR SPEECH AND LISTENING STYLES

Remember that in phone conversations your image rests almost entirely upon how well you manipulate your speech. Given this fact, be mindful of your telephone tone and habits. To determine your patterns, tape yourself throughout a few conversations. (*If directly recording both ends of a conversation, however, be sure to abide by any legal stipulations that may apply.*) Note what words you use. How are your volume, tone, rate, pitch, pronunciation, and enunciation? Do you listen respectfully and attentively—without frequently interrupting the other party? How well do *you* handle interruptions? These are all important contributors to someone's perception of your image. It doesn't matter if you think you "got it goin' on." What the other party *hears* and *feels* during a phone conversation is what matters.

That's why it is important to mirror what you've heard when you're listening to someone over the phone. Don't let people's inability to express themselves clearly and well the first time around be a hindrance to your connecting with the issue at hand. It's a bit like defensive driving. You've got to "look out for the other guy" as well as for yourself. Thus, it follows that you need to repeat, rephrase, or review what you and the other party have said during a conversation—particularly at the end of it—so that both you and the other person have the same understanding of what has been discussed.

TECHNIQUE MATTERS

To have greater success with receiving calls, practice the following tips. First, before you even reach for the receiver, sit up straight and SMILE. You will be surprised as to just how much this can help you set the tone for a successful conversation. (The same goes for making calls.) Second, bear in mind that your handling of the first ten seconds of the conversation usually determines whether a caller likes, trusts, or wishes to continue to talk to you. So, nail those critical seconds!

Fill them with professional courtesy and competence by clearly thanking the person for calling, then stating the name of your company or department, identifying yourself, and asking how you may be of assistance. For example, say "Thank you for calling Artison Associates, this is Iris or Ms. Dawson. How may I help you?" Since people like to be recognized (and generally react favorably when they are) make a point of *remembering the caller's name.* Jot it down if possible and ask for the correct spelling of it if you are unsure—especially when you're taking a message for someone else. Then, unless it's a really brief conversation, use the person's name at least once. This suggests a certain level of caring and consideration.

AVOID "ON-HOLD" LIMBO AND TRANSFER TORTURE

If you are too busy to take the call immediately, ask the person if he *minds* holding and—here's the kicker—WAIT TO HEAR THE PERSON'S RESPONSE. Or, to avoid having to wait for a response or being rude and automatically placing the individual on hold, simply say, "Please hold." That way you are not asking a question that compels a response. You are making a polite request.

After returning to the caller (which should be *no longer than 30-45 seconds*), please thank the person for holding, then proceed to hear the request or comment. If callers must remain on hold for much longer than 45 seconds, give them the option of continuing to hold or leaving a message. DO NOT LEAVE THEM IN "ON-HOLD" LIMBO. That is simply rude and shows no regard for the importance of someone else's time.

Next, if you must transfer a call. Don't just click the person over without acknowledging that you are about to do so. Say something like, "Please hold while I transfer you" or "It'll be my pleasure to connect you, please hold." Little things like that mean *everything* to callers in our fast-paced-don't-have-time-for-you society. You never know who is on the other end of the line. You could make someone's day with just that bit of courtesy. Or, you could plant a positive impression in the caller's mind that distinguishes both you and your company or organization. And you never know what harvest that might bring in somewhere down the line.

MONITOR YOUR ENERGY AND ENTHUSIASM

Always be positive and sound energetic. Even though you may sound lively enough in person, usually when we speak into machines of any sort, a certain percentage of our personal energy falls off due to the technology. So, be conscious of sounding enthusiastic. However, don't overdo it.

Monitor your volume and rate. While usually a person will tell you if she can't hear you, that's not a cue to start yelling. Instead, simply make sure you are properly directing your voice into the receiver. As far as your pace is concerned, generally, you should adjust how fast or slow you talk to how fast or slow the caller is speaking. This will subconsciously make the caller feel more at ease and more comfortable with talking to you.

Be particularly attentive when listening to and responding to persons for whom English is a second language. Use a little empathy. What if you were in the same situation? Often, it's not easy and sometimes it can be downright frustrating. Therefore, be careful not to use long words unnecessarily. And above all else—be patient.

DEFUSE AN UPSET CALLER

One of the most crucial times to exercise patience, a cornerstone of professionalism, is when you are dealing with an upset party on the other end of the line. Remember, your goal is to make and maintain a positive connection no matter how angry or frustrated the other person may be.

To begin with, detach yourself *personally* and immediately move into your ultra-professional mode. Say to yourself, *'This person is mad about* **a situation** *and not about* **me** *personally.'* That is, unless you know you have done something to warrant such retaliation. And if *that's* the case...well that's another whole lesson. Anyway, be committed up front to hearing the person out (within reason). Listen carefully to establish the real source of the person's anger. Yes, you should listen long enough to pick up on the chief complaint, but you *do not* have to entertain a tongue-lashing that seems as if it could go on indefinitely.

As soon as you hear the problem, move quickly to defuse the

person's anger so that you can begin to work swiftly towards a point of resolution. After all, it is in both parties' best interest for you to short-circuit anger so you can get at working out the issue at hand. You might be able to nip it in the bud, so to speak. First, acknowledge how the person must feel. Then, use the mirroring technique to restate the facts of the situation as you have heard them. Most of the time when people are explosive, it's because they feel they have been abused or mistreated in some fashion. It is amazing how often ego enters into the equation. People tend to become offended rather quickly when they feel they've been over-looked, ignored, or not really listened to.

So, let them know that you can imagine that (*whatever the situation is*) must have caused them to become upset. Doing so allows you to get their attention and let them know that you are *not* the enemy and that you are genuinely concerned. For example, you might say, "I can imagine how frustrated you must be not to have gotten what you ordered."

Next, when the caller responds (usually in a somewhat calmer tone), you can lead him to tell you what he needs or wants that can "make the situation right." It doesn't matter if you feel his concern is unjustified. Complainers often feel to the very core of their be-ing that not only is their position justified but that you or someone in your company or organization had *some nerve* treating them badly. In business, the complainer's perception, or point of view, is all that matters to him. Therefore, don't try to stand toe-to-toe and get embroiled in a slugfest of mean-spirited words with an upset caller. Remember, the callers are not your personal opponents, nor are you theirs.

COUNT THE CALL AS A BLESSING

Work to achieve a solution in which you come out looking good even when the caller thinks someone has stepped on her toes and caused her extreme discomfort. You may feel it is a matter of supreme inconvenience to be tied up on the phone with a disgruntled individual. But wouldn't you prefer that the person let *you* know about the problem rather than 11 *other* people? (Statistics show that a dissatisfied person will seek to "infect" an average of 11 people with dislike for you if a problem is not resolved quickly).

So, do the miraculous—actually COUNT IT A BLESSING when someone calls you to lodge a complaint. At least it gives you the opportunity to be aware of perceptions—whether they are based in reality or are figments of someone's imagination.

SINCERELY FOCUS ON THE CALLER'S NEEDS

After you have placed the angry caller at ease and transformed him into a human again, you can focus on what requests, wants or needs he may have. Assess them and formulate a plan of positive response. Actually ask the caller, what he would like for you to do to remedy the situation.

Be sure to avoid referring to the individual as someone with a "problem." This is when an appreciation for the power of effective diction can really come in handy. Instead, try referring to the caller's "situation," "concern," or "experience." Speak in positive tones about how you want his future experiences with you to be satisfying. And, by all means, *be genuine.* Don't sound like you're dishing out canned baloney. Sincerity can win over even the angriest caller while even a hint of fakery can fuel his disgust.

Next, actually listen to and maybe even jot down the person's requests. Then, outline for him exactly what you *can* do. And remember, too many "rescued" phone calls have gone sour again near the end because "the accused," in an honest effort to lay out her limits, simply chose the wrong words or tone to do so.

Using any negatives, either in tone or speech, at this point, can be totally counterproductive. Why after spending the time to build a bridge of goodwill would you want to torpedo it with a negative? For instance, if the person is demanding to come in personally and speak with you to further, and hopefully finally, resolve the situation at a time that is impractical, inconvenient or impossible for you, DO NOT say, "Oh no, I'm not the person you need to speak to." *OR*..."I'm sorry, but I can't see you on Saturdays; we're closed." *OR* "One o'clock is our busiest time of the day; I can't possibly meet with you then." Instead, tell him WHAT YOU *CAN* DO. For example, "I'd be happy to meet with you on Thursday at 2:00." Or, name the individual who *can* help and indicate that you will check with that person and get back with the caller *at a specific time* with an appointment date and time.

Then, before hanging up, do yet another unthinkable thing: THANK THE PERSON FOR CALLING. I know, it may sound a little illogical, but focus with your long-range vision. You are striving to turn a dissatisfied person into a satisfied one. It may not feel right or good to thank an angry caller, but it is the professional thing to do. Lastly, be sure to *keep your word*! Either call back if that's what you said you would do, *or* keep the face-to-face appointment *or* do whatever the two of you have agreed upon to bring the matter to a swift positive end. This shows concern and integrity, both of which can have huge payoffs.

CONQUER PHONE JITTERS

"But *my* main problem is that I get a funny feeling in the pit of my stomach, or I get all nervous and sweaty right before I call someone on the phone to conduct any business. You see, deep down inside I'm afraid I'll sound stupid." Well, if this sounds like you, the wisest thing I can say is remember that you are a *competent* individual whose divine right is to proceed through this life with an unmistakable air of confidence!

You were not charged to walk around with or sit around in or speak from a spirit of fear. Second Timothy 1:7 tells us that God has given us a spirit of power and of a sound mind. Keep in the forefront of your mind the fact that you are practicing every day to be an excellent communicator. Besides, the person on the other end of the line has made her share of mistakes and probably won't notice if you slip up a bit or, at the very least, will be understanding.

If you are habitually nervous before placing business calls, here are a few quick guidelines. Write down and rehearse your questions or comments before you pick up the phone. And have your facts straight! Also, jot down and prepare your responses to any objections or criticisms the other party may have. Be committed to maintaining your assertiveness and courtesy no matter what. Sit up straight...SMILE and *go for it*!

There's an old Native American prayer that might be particularly calming as you work on your telephone skills...

To the Great Spirit, a Prayer:

"May you have the strength of eagles' wings,

The faith and courage to fly to new heights,

And the wisdom of the universe to carry you there."

Trust God to guide and strengthen you as you face the unknowns and tackle the uncertainties of handling business telephone calls, and rest assured that *things will turn out just fine.*

*"Go confidently in the direction of your dreams.
Live the life you have imagined."*
— Henry David Thoreau

Chapter 5

VERBAL CHARM
Strengthening Interview Skills

Why do so many people react to job interviews in much the same way that they react to a dentist's visit? *You* know, they tense up, break into a sweat, get a queasy feeling in their stomachs, and actually feel faint. Some may even clam up involuntarily. They literally become tightlipped, which is exactly the opposite of what the professionals they will be facing need them to do.

Not opening your mouth properly at a job interview makes about as much sense as barely parting your lips in a dentist's chair. Sure, in both settings you may be afraid that you will be drilled even more intensely if you open up too much. But the whole point of subjecting yourself to scrutiny in either case is to display your strengths and attend to any weaknesses. And, if handled well, you should emerge with a smile, confident that business has been managed effectively.

SELL YOUR EXPERIENCES

Interviewing for a job does not have to be an anxiety-filled process. With adequate preparation (knowledge and practice), you can perform well in any employment interview. Provided that your experiences and capabilities relate to the position you're seeking. Notice that I didn't correlate your interview performance with how much specific experience you've had that *precisely* matches the responsibilities in a given position description. Instead, the focus is on "experienc*es*," not "experience."

"Experience," in the job interview context, generally and rather routinely refers to the amount of time one has spent engaged in a specific set of job duties outlined by an employer either in writing or orally. However, the word "experienc*es*" suggests various encounters and situations that you, the position candidate, might draw upon and apply to whatever job circumstances in which you may find yourself.

In other words, if you can smoothly persuade interviewers that your experiences have prepared you to adapt to a range of circumstances, you can increase your chances of being seriously considered for hire. Even if your work history does not include direct experience in a particular field, if presented in the right light, your experiences can be seen to relate indirectly to a job the targeted organization may have available.

TURN COLD CALLS INTO HOT LEADS

If you are cold calling—pounding the literal or, in this computer-reliant age, the "virtual" pavement—and there are no apparent openings, you can package your capabilities so favorably that a position might be *created just for you.* Armed with extraordinary job search skills, you could even be hired to fill a need that an employer may not readily realize exists. Or, your "know-how" in meeting a challenge or handling a crisis that may have arisen suddenly could land you a job.

With industry competition getting stiffer every day, employers are perhaps more eager than ever to get ahead in the race to capture a greater market share—or to hold onto what they already have. And your skills and abilities could offer them just the competitive advantage they need. At the very least, smartly selling professional or occupational strengths can result in your résumé being retained for future reference should a position become available.

DEVELOP THE "GIFT OF NAB"

When done well, both informational and hiring interviews can distinguish you as someone worthy of immediate employment. Seasoned job seekers have been mastering them for years. They have consistently outdistanced other applicants by developing what I call "the gift of *nab*": the capacity to capture the attention of interviewers and create a strong, *positive* impression that elicits a job offer. Some of these master interviewers, in fact, get offers *over a year later*—and often *for even better jobs* than the ones originally sought!

This is neither fantasy nor fiction. And it could become *your* reality if you are willing to do what it takes to strengthen your interview skills. Just like virtuosos, world-class athletes, and accomplished actors, high-performance interviewees are *not* overnight successes. They are individuals who cultivate and fine-tune their techniques to the degree that, by comparison, others just don't quite measure up.

They are standard bearers who carry a torch of excellence so bright that others' efforts seem somewhat dim in light of theirs. They polish their skills so that they consistently manipulate outcomes to their favor. Now, this does not imply negativity or deception. By "manipulate," I simply mean they reshape, redevelop or refashion interviews so that they are given the opportunity to shine *respectfully.*

A great way to condition yourself to answer and ask questions during an interview is to practice your roles in general conversation scenarios, like those in *Study Guide F* (pp. 114-116). This guide also lists some frequently asked general interview questions.

EXERCISE YOUR OPTIONS

'Now,' you may wonder, *'how in the world can an interviewee "manipulate" an interview in a positive manner?'* *'I always thought that the interviewer had the upper hand.'* That is true, however, ultimately *you* are in control of the information you reveal in an interview.

A pretty good analogy is to compare yourself to the driver of a bumper car at an amusement park. While how long the ride lasts and its boundaries are under someone else's control, you do have the freedom to steer, accelerate, slow down, and swerve to avoid collisions. The same thing is true in an interview situation. The employer is in control of how long the interview lasts and most of the territory to be covered. But you *do* have options. Once you determine the needs of the organization (such as their major challenges), you can steer the conversation in directions that cast you in a favorable light, highlighting what you believe you can do for the employer.

HANDLE PROBLEM INTERVIEWERS

The beauty of being well prepared for interviews is that you can "rescue" a discussion if the interviewer goes astray *or* stagnates. Whether he detours significantly from typical main topics or gets hung up on a point, you can refer to a mental map of where you desire the interview to go. This is useful because, frankly, some interviewers are not that good. Their weaknesses may hamper the interview and never allow you to get around to the areas of discussion that reflect your strong suits.

So, actually map out on a sheet of paper: (1) key points you intend to make, (2) important information you want to share, and (3) specific supporting details you might offer as solid examples. Then, memorize what you want to say. Next, practice paraphrasing your statements. Being able to discuss your strengths in several different ways can keep you from sounding robotic. And it can lessen your chances of going blank if you happen to flub or forget a word or two. In short, preparation helps words flow more naturally. Especially when you're hedged in by a runaway or a "surface" interviewer.

When an interviewer rambles seemingly for miles off track, your goal and responsibility to yourself is to craftily nudge the discussion away from winding, bumpy, and often twisted back roads and get it back onto the Interstate, so to speak, so you can resume a smoother, swifter course to your destination. Your mission is to tell him just what you want him to know about you and why you are the ideal candidate for the job. However, in your zeal to be impressive, be sure to stay in your place. Don't take over the interview by *forcing* the discussion to fit your map. Simply, be patient and watch for opportunities to unfold for you to inject your points. If you don't get the chance to do so during the session's prime time, don't despair. You might be able to slip them in during an end-of-interview summary statement. And if that doesn't happen, just stay collected and quietly confident.

Another type of "problem" interviewer is a rude or hostile one. What should you do if you find yourself backed against a wall by an impolite interrogator? First of all, never fire back with aggressive behavior or a sarcastic tone. Remember always to remain polite yourself and to keep a pleasant expression on your face and an agreeable tone in your voice.

Maintain assertive, though not aggressive, posture and eye contact throughout, even if you feel you are under attack. And be aware that the interviewer's "attack" really may not be an attack at all. Know that any sudden perceived aggression may be designed specifically to see "what stuff you're made of." Some interviewers actually like to add a little under-the-gun atmosphere to the mix, just to see how you will react to criticism or pressure. They may come up with potentially stress-inducing or challenging questions merely to simulate the actual work atmosphere and watch your reaction. So, relax and call on your positive mental image of yourself—confidently and successfully sailing through the interview.

What if an interviewer repeatedly questions you about a certain area? Does it mean she is obsessive or disorganized and has forgotten that the question already has been asked and answered? To the contrary, it is not uncommon for a highly-skilled interviewer to ask the same question more than once and in more than one way. Often this is done to test your depth and consistency. In all likelihood, the interviewer will be checking to see if you know that the question is a repeated one simply worded a little differently. She may be interested in seeing if your answer will remain the same, be totally different or change slightly, offering further details and examples.

To prepare for such an instance, anticipate key questions and practice your responses *long before the interview*. Vary the way you provide the same information. For example, you may be asked to give your greatest strength. Then, similarly, an interviewer may tell you to discuss your capabilities. Later still, you may be asked to detail your qualifications for the job in question. Essentially, these three questions may be set up strategically to get at the same information—perhaps on slightly different levels. With that in mind, your responses should contain the same core elements but feature a little something extra as you progress. Thus, your prime assets at a time like this will be listening carefully and having prepared thoroughly to give a variety of *coherent* responses.

DON'T PRETEND

Often a major temptation, especially when you're being pressed for deeper information, is to offer more "show" than you have "substance" to back up. So, no matter how inadequate you may feel when the pressure is on, DO NOT turn into The Great Pretender. Even if you really want the job but feel that you somehow are falling a bit short of the requirements as presented by the interviewers, don't begin to project an image that you have played in the Big

50

Leagues already when you know you only have a Pee Wee League background. BE HONEST because in the long run, you *will* be found out. Stick with what you actually know and have accomplished and assertively pledge to build upon that.

In other words, keep the expression "fake it 'til you make it" in proper perspective. Understand that, in these instances, it simply means you should have a constant mental picture of yourself as successful. You should project an attitude of confidence—without coming across as arrogant or cocky. And, certainly, you should not make false representations about your present level of competence. Instead, admit, in a positive way, any obvious relevant shortcomings in the light of a definite commitment to enhance your skills in due time.

Four Basic Interview Types

There are four major interview types: traditional, informational, telephone, and "fishing expeditions." To be well rounded, you should sharpen your skill in handling each.

The Traditional Interview

We are all most familiar with the traditional interview. You are invited to be interviewed by a single individual or a team (sometimes you won't know which is the case until you arrive and enter the interview room). The announced object of the meeting is to fill an advertised opening. Some questions are direct and require simple (though well-constructed) answers that you can back up with specific examples of your skills, qualifications, or experience. One really important factor in how well you do with such questions is how clearly and concisely you present your assets relative to the prospective employer's needs or expressed challenges.

Let's look at an example. If you are asked if you've had experience in management, you might say, *"During the five years that I worked for the Jones, Smith, & Thomas housewares distributor-*

ship, I was responsible for managing the assignments and duties of a staff of 14. While supervising three direct reports, I was able to ensure smooth operations in the accounting, purchasing, and marketing departments. " Now, that's a good deal better than answering *"yes"* or thinking you're really rolling along well by just including a version of the question in your answer and saying, *"Yes, I have five years of management experience."* While the latter answers do address the question, they don't add anything to your image as a communicator. So, even if a simple response is called for, remember—it's all about the packaging. Make sure that even your short answers allow you to shine.

Another kind of question commonly encountered in a traditional interview is the open-ended one. In other words, these are not yes-or-no questions. Because many interviewees don't realize that "open-enders" are wonderful opportunities to shine, they squander these chances to drive the interview for a while. So, prepare well to answer such questions. And when they are asked, be excited that the reins have been handed over to you temporarily, but don't "ride the horse to death." In other words, use the time wisely to showcase your merits, but don't go on too long. You may end up rambling too far and talk yourself right out of a job. Open-ended does not mean *un*ending.

For example, to test your knowledge of the industry, you may be asked to give your impressions of hot trends. You might pattern your response after the following technology example: *"Two of the hottest trends in computing today are electronically-projected presentation slides and personal digital assistants. Programs such as PowerPoint and Corel Presentations offer speakers-on-the-go incredible flexibility in terms of how much information can comfortably be shown and how much creativity can be applied. As far as PDA's go, their capacity to store, retrieve, and transmit information on the run has revolutionized both the computing and communications industries."*

This response indicates that you do, indeed, know something about two of the leading technological tools. You clearly established at the beginning of your response that you would discuss two items. Then you briefly discussed them knowledgeably. To determine whether or not you should go on, try reading the interviewer's body language. Sometimes changes in facial expression, as well as head and body movement, can provide clues. In fact, at times, many interviewers use these types of nonverbals instead of actual follow-up questions.

Once you've concluded such a discussion, your next step should be to smile and maybe even slightly nod—indicating that you're awaiting the next question. The key is to sufficiently, but economically, answer the question and *move on*. It's not that hard to apply these approaches to whatever interview subject is at hand. Just prepare and practice ahead of time. Remember...anticipate, anticipate, ANTICIPATE. The more prepared you are, the better you will handle this type of interview.

Gathering Information and Going Fishing

Informational and fishing expedition interviews are very much alike. Typically, the first is designed to uncover general industry or company facts. However, it could yield valuable specifics about possibilities for hire. The purpose of the second is simply to cast a broad net targeted at hauling in loads of hiring leads. You should handle them similarly. Since you will have been the person who initiated the contact, obviously, you will have more control over their content. These cold-call interviews allow you simply to test the waters to gather information about (1) a specific area of interest (2) specific position types or (3) actual job or contract opportunities related to your area of expertise.

Literally, you may walk in and request to meet with the person in charge of a particular department, such as computers, accounting, or marketing. Who knows? He might be free to entertain a few questions, so have them typed or written out before you show up. Then, *stick to them* unless you are invited to explore other areas by the person *you* are actually interviewing.

In the event your "interviewee" has very limited time to talk to you, at least state your intentions and try to arrange a brief future "fishing" interview. You will be surprised how often this works. Some people will welcome the interest and actually feel somewhat flattered that someone has requested an audience with them. In either case, plan on not taking up more than 30 minutes of the individual's time, and be sure he knows that up front. Then stick to that time frame. And remember, the more organized you are before you show up, the better the interview will flow—and the better you'll look!

The Telephone Interview

Usually, the telephone interview is predetermined and requested by a company that is scouting for recruits. Primarily, organizations use it for screening purposes. The interviewer's goals are to see how well qualified you are and how well you can express those qualifications. She will be checking your knowledge *and* your communication skills.

In this type of situation, you must remember that your voice and speech patterns are your greatest tools—along with any reference sheets (résumé, notes, etc.) you may have placed near the phone in anticipation of the interviewer's call. So, use them well. Smile and be energetic. Also, make sure any distractions are handled *before* you get into the thick of the interview. If you have to, politely ask the caller to hold for a moment. You may need to "turn down the volume" on not only the television, radio, noisy relatives or friends...*but on nervousness as well.* Just be sure not to keep the interviewer waiting for more than 15 or 20 seconds while you "compose your external and internal environments." Then, gather your wits and your interview tools, and do your thing!

ANSWERS TO HAVE READY

With all types of job interviews, be sure to have prepared answers about your strengths and your weaknesses. Be certain not to exaggerate your strong points. Simply, discuss them within the context of the job you are seeking. And even though you are discussing strengths, talk about them with appropriate professional modesty. In other words, showcase your assets, but don't paint a larger-than-life picture of yourself.

As for weaknesses, disclose pertinent ones that you can share in a positive light—for both you and the employer. Here are a couple of common examples: (1) being so dedicated to your assignments that you have a "bad" habit of coming in very early and staying over late to make sure all details are completed satisfactorily and (2) performing many tasks yourself, rather than delegating assignments, to ensure that they are done properly—although you're finding that, through excellent initial and follow-up communication, you're becoming more comfortable with allowing others to handle certain matters.

Also, be ready to answer questions about your short-term and long-range goals. To prepare, find out ahead of time (if possible) what jobs within the interviewing organization are one level and several steps above the one for which you are being considered. Then, tailor your answers along those lines—if indeed those positions interest you. And at this juncture rarely, if ever, is it safe to share any long-term plans about starting your own business or doing anything irrelevant to the industry being discussed.

HOW TO CLOSE

Experts suggest that you have at least two questions to ask at the end of an initial interview. They should reflect your knowledge of the company while still showing that you're not quite clear about how the business may manage specific operations or functions. *'Why bother?'* you ask. *'I'll just be grateful for making it through the whole thing without sounding idiotic. And I certainly don't want to come across as a show-off. So, why should I risk stirring up a wasps' nest?'*

Asking the "right" questions suggests that you've done your

homework and may be genuinely interested in the organization. However, there are some areas you should not bring up. HEADING THE LIST are questions about salary/wages or benefits, such as personal leave time, sick days and vacations. Asking about these is considered a definite indication that you are more concerned with what an organization can do for *you* rather than about what *you* can do for it. If interviewers are interested in you, either they will quote a pay range or they will ask you what salary or wages you expect. Generally, they will outline benefits packages at a later date over the phone or in a follow-up interview. Sometimes, though, an interviewer will ask you to give him an expected range. If you don't know what is appropriate for the position, company, or industry— simply ask about the organizational standard.

After a face-to-face interview, always end with a firm (though *not crushing*) handshake, good eye contact and a smile. Hopefully, just as you began. (In most circles, however, it is customary to shake hands in the beginning only if the interviewer offers his hand first). Then, thank him for his time and LEAVE. Don't mill around hoping for extra time or a tour. Just exit graciously.

By practicing these interview techniques, you should be full of *Verbal Charm* and see greater results from your job search endeavors. As a matter of fact, polished verbal skills can even attract job offers years afterwards—even when you aren't looking for a job. They really can help you become a job magnet. It's happened to many others (including me—*a number of times*) and it can happen to you as well!

*"Though we travel the world over to find the beautiful,
we must carry it with us or find it not."*
— Ralph Waldo Emerson

Chapter 6

ICING ON THE CAKE
The Power of Physical Image and Body Language

Whoever coined the expression "action speaks louder than words" obviously appreciated the strength of vision. Not deep insight or long-range imaging, simply "vision"—regular old "sight." Long before we open our mouths, others may make judgments about us purely based upon how we look to them and what we do. While this may be a plus at times, it can also work to our disadvantage.

According to a number of communication experts, roughly 93% of what we say is transmitted nonverbally. Therefore, our goal should be to use physical image, facial expressions, voice tones and body movements to enhance our chances of being received as we wish. In fact, by strategically managing your "look" *and* your actions, you can significantly boost your overall appeal. You can influence the opinions of others without ever *saying* one word! But then, this should not come as a surprise to anyone. We all send, receive, interpret and perceive "silent" messages every day. A classic reminder is the rather humorous quip "Don't you *look* at me in that tone of voice."

Just think back to how many times you yourself may have drawn conclusions about people because of their appearance alone. Odds are there was something about the person that stood out. Whether it was an attractive hair style, a striking smile, a repetitive motion or wrinkled clothing, there was something that got your attention. Something swayed your thoughts in either a positive or negative direction. Whatever the red flag *or* the gold star may have been, it made a lasting impression. The fact is—whether it's fair or not—people tend to believe what they *see* first, even if eventually something you say steers their minds down another path. And that can be good *or* bad *or* both.

MASTER IMAGE CHALLENGES

Exposed physical flaws can be huge communication barriers. If they can't be fixed or camouflaged, they can be particularly distracting or even send the wrong message. Potentially even more troublesome are instances where, in fact *or* perception, such flaws could have been avoided but weren't. Having such appearance glitches can be unnerving for both "the marred" *and* observers. Especially in cases of public speaking. However, rising above them can leave quite an amazing impression. (For tips on enhancing oral presentation physical presence, see *Study Guide G*, pp. 120-122.)

One of the most memorable examples of rising above an image bombshell involves one of my mentors, a fellow corporate trainer and motivational speaker. Years ago, I was a participant in one of her seminars. However, my first and strongest impression of her was formed before we ever met.

A colleague and I were sitting in a fairly well-populated lobby of a rather modest hotel waiting for the first session of a three-day leadership conference to begin...when This Amazing Stranger floa-oa-ted through the main entrance and up to the registration desk. I was so impressed with the woman's poise and gracefulness that I immediately remarked to my friend, "I don't know who she is, but she's 'SOMEBODY'...Just *look* at her." My friend (understanding that I was referring to the woman's overall appearance, carriage, and stance) quickly agreed. She too had been impressed.

Trying our best not to gawk or conspicuously eavesdrop, we continued to admire the confident-looking woman from a distance until she finally disappeared around a corner. Little did we know that she was there for the same conference we were attending—at which she (as it turned out) would be one of the presenters—and *an absolutely spellbinding one* at that.

The next day about mid-morning (after having had stereotypically "O.K." sessions the afternoon before and earlier that morning), about 25 other future and then-current organizational leaders and I sat in a conference room, preparing ourselves to politely "endure" yet another average presentation. Then, our host began to "prime the pump" for a warm reception of our second Day 2 trainer.

From the introduction alone, I knew we were in for a treat. That is, if the facilitator were to be believed. Then, as soon as he was done and the previous day's "mystery woman" stepped forward, I smiled and settled into my seat for what I just knew would be an inspirational ride. Oddly enough, while her credentials were supremely impressive, my great anticipation rested primarily on the strength of her *body language* THE DAY BEFORE. And, sure enough, throughout her presentation, the magnetic speaker lived up to the image she had so effortlessly projected.

From the moment Vera J. Hilliard took center stage, she captivated the group. At first, she did so simply by her commanding presence. Again, she seemed to glide into position. And within seconds, she *owned the entire room*! Her body language, as well as her verbal message, said that she, without question, was about "excellent" business. She was so mesmerizing that I felt she could do no wrong—at least not in her role as a speaker and teacher. That is, *until* I incidentally did a full-body scan.

I found myself beginning a "head-to-toer" and...you guessed it...she was TOGETHER (dressed nicely but *very* similarly to the way she was dressed the day before, I recalled). She was "together" all right...from head to *knee*, that is. That's right, I never got past her legs. Because there on *prominent* display (as they usually happen to be) were the BIGGEST, UGLIEST runs in her hose. They were, in fact, the worst that I had ever seen (at least *out in the open like that*)!

Not ONE, but BOTH legs of her hose were just short of being totally destroyed. And for the purposes of the setting we were in...they might as well have been. Because, ladies, we *know* the damage that just one SMALL run can do to most of our psyches in certain situations. Even though it may not actually ruin the nylon itself, it certainly can make us self-conscious. After all, we just KNOW that E-EV-ERYBODY is going to notice it right off and immediately lessen their opinion of us. Therefore, we learn very early on that extra hose and clear nail polish are *essentials* in any "self-respecting" *la*-dy's Appearance Emergency Kit, particularly in a professional setting. And gentlemen, if you have ever witnessed a woman practically "lose it" over a run, then you too know what I'm talking about.

But *that* day at *that* time, neither polish nor a spare pair of hose had been viable options for Vera (as we would all learn just prior to our midday break). To say I almost *gagge*d on the huge gasp I struggled to stifle when my eyes temporarily "locked on" to those runs would be only a slight exaggeration. The runs were more like rivulets and tributaries spreading all over the place, seeming to stretch far beyond the confines of the speaker's legs—even momentarily to overtake my brain! Like a boat meandering along a winding stream, my mind wandered restlessly as my eyes zigzagged from those runs to the speaker's mouth and back several times.

At first, my attention was split by the sheer shock of the discovery. I couldn't believe that such an accomplished, "together" woman had the nerve to stand before us in such a flawed fashion. Then, my concentration was broken precisely *because of* that tremendous nerve of hers. Soon my shock and distraction turned into dumbfoundedness. I was absolutely awestruck that this trainer could manage so easily to remain "in her element" with what she would later refer to as "railroad tracks" in her hose. Then, before I knew it, I was so deeply engrossed in *what* she said and *how* she said it that I was no longer aware of "THOSE HOSE."

You see, Vera was "POISE" personified. She was so self-assured, so self-possessed and articulate that nothing stopped her fluid nature. Nothing made her shrink behind a lectern and stand there planted and growing roots to hide such highly visible flaws. I mean...she showed *NO* shame. That was not only admirable. In *my* book, it fell just short of miraculous! Just think back to how often you've heard people apologize for *a lack of "this"* or *a touch of "that"* before giving a speech or singing a solo.

From the words that flowed off her tongue to the confidence that exuded from her body language, Ms. *Hill*iard was "on the mark." There was *no* calling her competence into question. She was prepared: to share what she knew and to bear what none of us knew (the circumstances surrounding her questionable appearance).

After a purely riveting two-hour ride, Vera finally coasted into cruise mode and smoothly redirected our trains of thought from her inspiring presentation to a lunchtime transition. Like a seasoned engineer, she indicated that she'd safely guided us to her desired destination—a midday break and a perfect opportunity for her to solicit aid in upgrading her appearance. Now, while the individual gasps upon discovery of The Nylon Ruins may have been swallowed, the collective sigh of relief at Vera's "confession" could have been compared to The Shot Heard Around the World.

With the same finesse that she had maintained throughout her formal presentation, the woman released her captive audience in more ways than one. First, she announced that we were free to go to lunch. Second, she coolly acknowledged (for all ears to hear) that her pantyhose looked deplorable. Then, unbelievably, she didn't stop there. She went on to proclaim that her hairstyle left a bit to be desired and that the suit she was wearing was the same one she had worn all the day before on her trek from Connecticut to Georgia (HENCE, THE FAMILIAR-LOOKING ENSEMBLE). Next, without missing a beat or making any apology, she proceeded to canvass the room for a replacement pair of pantyhose that matched to perfection her *café au lait* complexion. She also requested products and utensils to treat her hair with the loving care it deserved.

The girl had SOME nerve! And after she had finished her appeal, instantly, the outpouring of love, respect, and support was *un*real. From the *north*, *south*, *east*, and *west* emerged gift-bearing women, proving that Vera had passed the ultimate test. One after another, we filled her hotel room with helpful tokens that applauded her decision not to come "half-steppin' " into an obligation to impart knowledge and inspiration—all because a careless airline had lost her baggage.

That day, watching so many women, black and white alike, cross Vera's threshold was truly a sight to behold. As they came through the door delivering not only what she'd asked for...but *so much more*...I witnessed a remarkable move of fellowship that lasted throughout the day and well into the evening. I rejoiced at the sight of some of the most superficially different people (of both genders and many different backgrounds) being propelled together in support of a woman whose unbreakable spirit and charismatic attitude proved that no matter how bleak the circumstances may appear, your voice *and* body can project just *the right talk*.

By the way, if Vera had wanted to, the evening before she could have shopped 'til she dropped at any mall near the area. After all, she lives in a mansion and has a mind-blowing client portfolio (including past service to George H.W. Bush, Bill *and* Hillary). And the questions have been asked, "Why didn't she take a fashion 'emergency kit' (with a spare pair of hose) on the plane when she set out for Georgia?" "Why didn't she just go barelegged?"

In response to the first, Vera says that she is confident that even if the spare items she packs in her *checked luggage* don't arrive at her destination when she does, GOD WILL SUPPLY HER EVERY NEED in one form or another. In short, she has immense confidence in herself and *supreme* reliance upon her faith in God. And, between the two, she continues to move towards greatness and goes about the business He has assigned her. With God's help she consistently turns "lemons into lemonade." Therefore, she never has to settle for the bitter when she knows that, through faith and action, somehow life always can be sweet. Now, *that's* AWESOME...and what's more...THAT PHILOSOPHY NEVER FAILS TO WORK.

As for the second question, Vera categorically declares that being barelegged—even under such extenuating circumstances—would have been in poor taste in that setting. So would have, she says, making any introductory apologies for her appearance either with The Nylon Ruins or with bare legs.

Just think! What are the odds that a roomful of people would practically fight over who would drive, sit next to, and dine with a *railroad-pantyhose-tearing, same-old-suit-wearing* woman who didn't understand that the safest thing for her would've been to remain hidden behind a lectern or tucked under a hotel room bed...since the earth wouldn't oblige and swallow her up instead.

I believe that somewhere, probably in Vera's subconscious, she knew that someone would "get it"...that *someone* would learn something from her dilemma. I know that perhaps the greatest lesson *I* learned that day had nothing to do with the dynamic verbal teaching Vera had been hired to deliver. For me, the most penetrating lesson was one that, I believe, can stand right with Newton's law of gravity. In other words, it is an immutable, unchanging, abiding truth.

That day, Vera taught us all, through her very presence and actions, about the transcendent gravitational pull of a positive attitude. She proved that by displaying a powerfully confident and giving nature, no matter *how* things look, you can draw greatness to you. With the help of fruitful body language, you can reap harvests even when the fields appear to be infertile!

So, even when things go wrong, keep your head held high. Don't get snagged or snared by the dream killers, *Why Me?* and *Why Now?*

Just be committed to, as the old saying goes, "runnin' on and seein' what the end's gonna be" anyway and anyhow. When things go wrong as they sometimes will, just remember Vera's Lesson—*Don't stand still.* Let your body do the talking to get you over the hump. After all, you're no Forrest Gump...life is *not* "like a box of chocolates." You'll get...what you EXPECT, WANT and NEED. If you just keep acting like it's yours, it will be yours indeed.

PHYSICAL IMAGE AND BODY LANGUAGE REMINDERS AND POINTERS

Hygiene, Grooming & Dress

No matter where you are or what you're doing (outside of the private and intimate confines of your home), always be conscious of your physical presence. Because, as poet John Donne wrote, "No man is an island, entire of itself..." Unless you move to a desert island, you *will* be interacting with others. And no matter if you're T-shirt-and-jeans casual or evening-wear formal, the way you look and act can help or hurt you. Did you know researchers have found that *within seven seconds* of seeing you, people form an impression of you?

Given this widespread 7-second assessment, there are two indisputable physical image areas that we all should adhere to—CLEANLINESS and NEATNESS. They always count. So, first of all, monitor yourself for stains, wrinkles, dandruff and yes...the *unspeakables*, breath, body and clothing odor. Don't try to mask these beneath mouthwash, mints and strong cologne. Instead, deal with "the root" of any problems. Give proper attention to general and oral hygiene. And, by all means, if you are the least bit unsure about any of these, PLEASE ask someone to alert you about any problems with them. Also ask for help in finding solutions should you need it. Just be sure your helper is someone who, you think, will be honest with you.

In addition, you should address any cosmetic dental concerns that could be drawbacks, such as missing, broken or badly discolored teeth. Guard against dry lips and skin as well. And keep your nails clean, neat, and at a length and style that is acceptable for your profession (*or* for the one you desire).

Secondly, as far as hair is concerned, ladies and gentlemen, it's really very simple. Find an attractive *'do* that's right for *you* and when you do—keep it clean and properly done. And gentlemen, if you are not sporting a clean-shaven look, be sure any facial hair is neatly trimmed. (This includes periodically checking for "stray" nose and ear hairs.) And if you could use some help adjusting or managing your hair, visit a salon or shop with cosmetologists or barbers skilled at creating and maintaining professional styles.

A few words of caution though…In most professional arenas, for women, "big" *and* "tall" hairstyles are frowned upon, or at the very least considered undesirable. Likewise, for men, sometimes full beards are not preferable. And in many industries, notwithstanding talent, routinely some of "the best and brightest" have been pigeonholed because of trendy or even ethnic coifs and headdresses. Although we live in a multicultural society, corporate America, in particular, has been slow to embrace any look that "clashes" with its standards. Also, for certain government positions and even a number of jobs in small private companies, some hairstyles (extreme hemlines and ill-fitting clothing too) simply are considered unacceptable.

Next, remember that, as a matter of habit, you should avoid loud colors and flashy fabrics when it comes to conservative business settings. Especially in interview situations and most corporate offices, subdued dress is the rule of thumb. (This goes for clothing types, cuts and fabric patterns also.) In these settings, color-wise, safe bets (such as darker blues, browns, grays and black) always win for men *and* women's suits. In recent years, though, moderate jewel tones have become favorites of a number of female executives. And muted shades of just about any color not only work well for women in most cases, but are giving men welcome breaks from the "obligatory" white shirt. Just remember that some hues may flatter your skin tone, or coloring, better than others.

More and more, however, an array of vibrant colors have been making their way into women's business apparel lines, with the red ("power") suit being especially popular. Still, regardless of your gender, in most instances it's a good idea to wait until you establish yourself on a job before boldly broadening your wardrobe's color palette. To introduce splashes of color in the meantime, use shirts, blouses, ties, handkerchiefs or scarves. Corporately, of course, women have a good deal more latitude in this area. Even so, ultimately, what color you choose and how much you dress up or down largely depends on the position you're seeking (and any you aspire to), company/industry standards, and the setting (including the season and region of the country).

Next, ladies...be sure your undergarments are appropriate and all clothing attachments are in their proper places and *unseen*. Be especially careful about bra and slip straps, clothing hanger loops (which experts advise should be cut out as soon as you get the garment home), shoulder pads, and labels. No, it's not a sin if any of these are out of place, but they surely can mar the smoothness of your image.

Unless your goal is to cause an unforgettable stir—when wearing unlined dresses or skirts, it pays to wear a slip, adjusting its length, style, and color to complement your outfit. Pay close attention to aligning splits with any in your garments (which should be "setting appropriate"). Also, depending on the style, fabric weight, and fit of skirts, dresses and pants, mask or get rid of panty lines. One option, if the style suits you and you're wearing a dark color, is a thong. For pants, close-fitting dresses or skirts that are light-colored, wear dark or flesh-toned panties or pantyhose. And to avoid the risk of a supreme distraction, please stick with solid patterns. After all, you, as I once heard a woman implore, don't want to "walk around with see-through pants on and a 'Jumping Bunnies' print on your behind."

And both men and women, if you simply *must* walk around with your most treasured, most comfy, most "holey" undergarments on, please wear dark outer clothing because *no one else* wants to see them—or worse—WHAT THEY *MAY NOT* BE COVERING so well. Then, there's the whole issue of whether or not you choose to wear undergarments at all. While for some women going bra-less may be more a matter of taste and acceptability rather than support, going panty-less crosses over into the realm of hygienic concern (if you're not wearing pantyhose). A similar situation exists for men. Choosing not to wear an undershirt is not a crime. But in formal business settings, certainly, you should wear one under any light-colored, lightweight shirt—especially if your chest is hairy. And briefs and boxers, again, address hygiene.

Appropriate Makeup and Accessories

Ladies, for a "more together" and elongating look, color match "good" hose or socks with *good* shoes and, if at all possible, with pants, dress or skirt. That is, if you don't wear "neutral" colors. And, men, don't feed the male colorblindness stereotype; be sure to match sock color with trouser or shoe color—unless you are trying to be trendy.

Two other important areas are makeup and jewelry. Both of these can speak volumes about you. If you wear them at all, remember that with both, in traditional business settings, typically LESS is MORE.

Ladies, in broad daylight (outside of a photo shoot, video broadcasting or recording situation), *do not* apply makeup heavily. You don't want to run the risk of looking like a clown or as if you're stepping out for an evening on the town. In fact, in many instances, nothing beats a fresh, clean, blemish-free natural look—in both men *and* women.

Also, *do not* adorn every finger with a ring or turn your wrists into bracelet showcases. (Remember, traditionally, *less* is more.) Also, ankle bracelets are not standard corporate accessories. And if you wear earrings, they should be of modest size and design in most professional settings. As for men and earrings—even a single piercing can block your being hired at certain businesses or stall your climb up some corporate ladders. The same applies to visible neck chains. For both men and women, "more unconventional visuals," such as gold teeth, nose, brow, tongue and multiple ear piercings, carry similar risks. Likewise, in conservative settings, tattoos are taboo and should be concealed.

You might be wondering, *'Well what if I only wear or show them publicly away from the job?'* You see, too many people underestimate the impact that their away-from-the-job public appearance can have on their work image. The fact is you can boost or tank your reputation both *on* and *off* the clock. Many bosses operate on a 24-hour image clock. They believe your appearance and performance on the job and away can promote *or* jeopardize business. How often do we hear about employees losing their jobs because of "unfit" or "reckless" off-premises *behavior*. Legal or not, such firings still happen. Rarely, however, does any employer let it be known that "unprofessional" *looks* on employees' "private" time can cost them their jobs. Again, such terminations do occur—usually disguised as something altogether different.

You certainly have the right to follow your convictions about self-expression in word, action, and style. It's just that sometimes your perceived rights and company policies or unwritten expectations may not mix. So, when it comes to your private time…*you* decide…*to be* or *not to be* hired, promoted or fired…*"THAT* is the question."* If you're the least bit unsure about the answers (what is and is not considered acceptable in a given work setting or organization), ASK a supervisor or experienced associate whom you can trust to give you accurate information. And should you ever feel your legal rights (concerning on-premises and "off-the-clock" appearance) are being violated, by all means consult an attorney with expertise in handling personnel issues.

Even if you already do a good job of putting together your look, there is nothing wrong with seeking expert enhancement every now and then. So, for other tips on hygiene, dress and grooming, you may refer to a variety of sources, including books, magazines, tapes, style shows and Internet sites. And if you really want to "go over the top," treat yourself to a session with an image consultant. After all, DON'T YOU DESERVE THE BEST?!

Body Language Boosters

And now a final word about body language. Clearly, a general rule is that the setting dictates how casual or open your body language should be. Whatever you do, don't discount the power and effect that your nonverbal communication can have—as evidenced by the Astounding Vera story. Just imagine how differently her presentation (and that whole situation) could have turned out if she had not approached it with the right mindset and body language.

Again, there are numerous resources on the subject of body language and nonverbal communication. But here are a few reminders and tips:

1. *Energy* and *a pleasant facial expression* are key. Make them a priority. If you are a laid-back person who finds it a challenge to put pep in your step and grace on your face...then, in these instances, FAKE IT UNTIL YOU MAKE IT. Practice and study others who have what the French call "Je ne c'est quoi" (or that special something), then try to energize yourself *until you succeed*. Remember that low energy and an unpleasant or dull look is often equated with lack of confidence and questionable intelligence. So, even though you may be a winner, you may look and move like a loser.

2. *Eye contact* and *eye movement* are critical factors in how others perceive you. Have you heard the expression about the eyes being the windows of the soul? Well, if yours are always shifting and restless or watching the floor, ceiling or some distant object, you're probably advertising a pretty shabby display in your life's showcase. You may be sending undesirable messages. In American culture, establishing and respectfully main-

taining eye contact with others is a valued conversational skill. If you struggle in this area because of cultural differences or shyness, work on improving because definitely you will be sending a negative signal. People may sense that you're afraid or disinterested—whether you are or not. So, be mindful of this fact and make adjustments when necessary. Look into others' eyes when you're talking *or* listening. However, don't unnerve people by maintaining a "catatonic" stare or appearing to glare. Remember, as in all communications matters, balance is key.

3. *In multicultural situations*, especially dealing with individuals from other countries, *using and reading body language appropriately* is critical. Did you know that in certain foreign cultures some of the simplest everyday hand signals we use in America are considered insulting? For example, in Ghana the all-American "thumbs up" sign is absolutely obscene. So, studying *kinesics* (the science of how body and facial movements communicate) can prevent embarrassing incidents—particularly when you're dealing with foreign nationals.

4. *Be sure to stand and sit erectly.* That's right...STRAIGHTEN UP RIGHT NOW...sit or stand *tall*. Good posture gives you an edge, and poor posture can signal messages inconsistent with your high goals. If you want to get your life out of a slump or never get into one in the first place, set your mind on standing tall—figuratively and literally. Doing so consistently will position you to improve in so many areas of your life.

5. *Be conscious of proximity.* That is, in both business and social settings, maintain distances appropriate for your level of familiarity with others—individually. Do not try to coast along on a friend's close relationship with someone whom you hardly know.

Here's a quick lesson in *proxemics* (the study of interpersonal space). Observe the rules of the following four zones:

INTIMATE ZONE - Each person's "invisible bubble," extending outward from 16-18 inches from one's skin (from head to toe). Generally, reserved for "intimates"—immediate or very familiar extended family and really close friends. If you do not fall into either category, enter someone else's intimate space *BY INVITATION ONLY!*

PERSONAL ZONE - A space of 1½ to 4 feet extending outward from an individual. Typically reserved for good friends and close acquaintances.

SOCIAL ZONE - An excellent distance (4 to 12 feet) to maintain at business and social gatherings with new acquaintances (often dependent upon the activity or event).

PUBLIC ZONE - Rarely should strangers cross this line (over 12 feet) and camp inside any other zone—notable exceptions being in elevators, on crowded walkways and in public seating areas. This distance is customary for oral presentations. In most cases, the speaker should begin at and maintain such a distance for the bulk of a presentation.

Any deviation from these standards could signal a number of messages, either inviting *or* repelling. So, monitor others *and* yourself. Also, remember to take into account group differences in physical expression, e.g., male/female, young/old, and ethnic/international.

Continually monitoring the nonverbal messages you are sending and receiving can attract or block your blessings. So, dedicate yourself to aligning your body and appearance with standards that suit your goals. Strive daily to maximize your physical presence so that it works *for*, and not against, you.

> "Whether you believe you can do a thing or not,
> you are right."
>
> — Henry Ford

Chapter 7

BELIEVE YOU CAN FLY
The Power of Belief, Positive Self-Talk, and Persistence

Personally, I *do* believe that I can fly—above trials and tribulations—to reach the heights of my God-ordained destiny. I know that each of us has been placed on this planet to execute and fulfill a purpose that glorifies our *very* creation and by extension (and more importantly) our Creator. Thus, right communication, which is vital to achieving purpose, should remain among our highest priorities.

BATTLING ASSAULTS ON DIVINE GREATNESS

Life itself is a complex series of opportunities to surmount challenges to the greatness of your existence. Do you know that with every breath and heartbeat you have the glorious option of recognizing that the essence of your being is to mirror the awesomeness of God? Armed with that knowledge, how can you doubt your worth and capabilities?

Unfortunately, doubting yourself is not too terribly hard to do in a society that glorifies and commercializes negativity. From newspaper and television headlines to movie sound bites, "the negative" seems to steal the show just about always. With a continual bombardment of negativity, there is no wonder so many of us sell others *and* ourselves short. Our minds are almost always under attack. Thus, too many people don't have to wait for somebody else to put them down; they trip up *themselves* often enough by throwing stumbling blocks of self-doubt and negative self-talk at their own feet.

V.I.P. CONVERSATIONS

To make the world a better place, we all need to embrace the RIGHT TALK. So, it's essential to become comfortable with speaking properly to *the most important* person you can find anywhere. Now, you might say, "That sounds pretty *illogical*. Why on earth would I want to start at the top? Anyone who has ever climbed a flight of stairs knows you have to start at the bottom. Surely, you can't expect me to start with kings, queens and presidents; I need to start *small*. After all, you have to crawl before you walk, right? Everybody's got to start somewhere...right?"

Why have we been persuaded so easily that SOMEWHERE has to be small? Talking right begins with facing and embracing the strongest earthly voice you will ever encounter in your life. It starts with recognizing the power of the strongest human voice you have ever heard. No, it is not Martin Luther King's. It is not John F. Kennedy's. It is not your father's or your mother's, your boss's, your pastor's or any other's. The strongest voice you have ever heard is the voice you have heard the most. It is the one that's most familiar. It's the *one* voice you cannot escape—no matter where you turn. No matter how many voices surround you, it is the one that rises above all others.

Yes...that voice is *yours*. Immediately, you might think, *'But I don't have a booming voice...my voice is sort of small* or *it's definitely not that impressive* or *I don't talk very much at all—so what do you mean?'* Stop. Just listen to yourself. *That* was the voice. And you heard it loud and clear. Right there inside your head.

The strongest "natural" voice you will ever hear is your Inner Voice, the one that God created in you. It is the vocal "cord" that ties you to a higher place in this life. It is housed in a most incredible vehicle, divinely designed to carry you from birth to death like no other—your *mind*. Therefore, before you can begin to address strengthening your physical voice and making verbally sweet music, exercising melodious vocal "chords," you have to move to the Thought Realm—to your true Command Center.

MANAGE YOUR MIND

You see, you *are* a spirit living in a body governed by your Soul, which is composed of your mind, your will, your emotions, your intuition and your intellect. In American culture, we tend to use the word "mind" (a component of the soul) to represent the whole. That is, we use "the mind" to refer to all five elements: the mind (or general thought factory), the will (or desire base), the emotions (or feelings post), the intuition (or compass center) and the intellect (or capacity command).

Even though your "soul is in control," like any vehicle, it can be steered in a multitude of directions, and it can carry you only as far as its condition allows. In other words, how you manage your mind determines how far you climb. The familiar expression "it's all in your head" is rooted and grounded in the belief in the awesome power of the mind. In fact, the mind is the most astounding natural creative force on the planet. Everything your senses perceive (what you see, hear, touch, taste, and smell) began in either the mind of God or in the mind of man.

So, whatever circumstances exist in your life today and whatever situations arose in the past are primarily the reflections, the manifestations, of thoughts. Essentially, all things have their origin in the mind. Since experts have scientifically determined that a person's life moves in the direction of his most dominant thought, your mind has the power to take you from the valley to THE MOUNTAINTOP…and back again.

It's all up to you. If you want to get your life on a different track, exercise the glorious free will that the Creator gave you. Make the conscious decision to shape, mold, and maintain full control over your mind.

JUST BELIEVE

Your dreams are there for the asking…if only you believe. And paraphrasing Einstein's popular saying, "You *can* achieve ANYTHING that you conceive if you believe…and *Believe*…and **BELIEVE.**

Now take a moment to jot down the word "BELIEVE" in large letters. The largeness of the letters indicates just how big this concept actually can become in your life. If you are truly committed to becoming a stronger communicator…if you are actually serious about infusing your world with the *right talk*, then this concept of "believing" has to loom large in your everyday life.

If at first you don't succeed…check to see just how much you believe in whatever you are trying to accomplish. Make sure that YOU are not the one holding *you* back. Then press forth and try, try, try again. And should you continue to meet rejection, find comfort in the fact that it simply could be a reflection of a problem that has very little, if anything, to do with you.

Also, if you ever feel your hopes sinking, know that you can always rely on your *thinking* to turn your circumstances around. Through using the *right talk*, you can pick yourself up when you have been knocked down and have seen your dreams dashed against the ground. Always know that you can pick up the pieces and put your hopes, aspirations and vision back together again. You are not Humpty Dumpty, so stop looking to men to put the pieces of your fragmented life back in their proper places. That is *your* responsibility. And, with the help of The Almighty Potter, it's possible—no matter how shattered you might be. Life truly does go in the direction of your most dominant thought. So, THINK yourself whole, TALK yourself whole and you *WILL BE* whole! With God's help, you can rebuild and reshape yourself for a glorious future.

RULE YOUR SPIRIT & GUARD YOUR HEART

With each day's gift of life, you should make a conscious effort to view any negatives not as traumatizing, but as transformational. Cling to the promise of there being a silver lining behind each of life's storm clouds.

You must have the heart and spirit of a champion, being able to see yourself (through the power of creative visualization) as victorious. Even when circumstances are bleakest, you must press on. Though you may bend, don't bow and break under the pressure of outside influences and suggestions that cast you in a negative light. Maintain control of your mind, your spirit *and* your heart. Proverbs 25:28 states, "Whoever has no rule over his own spirit is like a city broken down, without walls." And Proverbs 4:23 says, "Keep your heart with all diligence, for out of it spring the issues of life."

So, remember that a strong mind fortifies your spirit, enabling you to block the invasion of negative suggestions that can nest in your heart. Know that being ruled by feelings born of someone else's opinion makes you vulnerable to continual manipulation. And allowing someone to manipulate you makes you no better off than a puppet on a string. Up when someone else validates that you're up...And down when someone else puts you down.

You're no marionette! Your time here on earth to honor the purpose for which God distinctly made you is much too short for you to operate under someone else's dominion. Certainly, we must adhere to the established rules of authority that will cause us to be blessed. However, *nobody* is called to be wholly dependent upon the whims and frivolous dictates of any earthly individual. GOD

GAVE YOUR MIND TO YOU. Your spirit belongs to you. Your spirit *is* you. When you allow anyone else to overrun it, you risk ruin—which is *not* your destiny. You risk having your heart's treasure corrupted.

SEIZE THE PROMISES OF VICTORY

Flood your mind with positive thoughts. Stay in fellowship with others who are likeminded and successful. Have no extended fear of failure. Simply acknowledge that setbacks will come. And when they do, seek the divine lessons they are bound to hold. Don't wallow in defeat. Battles, mishaps, heartaches, and pains may come, but you can be victorious. Even if you can't see it while the smoke is still thick and you are crying so much that you may make yourself feel sick, know that Ultimate Victory is yours.

Remember that everything you see, hear, touch, smell or taste ultimately owes its creation to a thought. And your thoughts? YOU control. You are a master builder, a consummate craftsperson, reflective of God. So, be diligent in your designing and refashioning of your life in the wake of setbacks and storms. Do not allow fear to drown your dreams. Don't let what others may think, say, or do dull your vision. The Almighty has victory set aside in matters concerning you. *That*—you've got to believe.

And in your quest to use the *right talk*—your brilliance can be far greater than that of the phoenix (a mythological desert-dwelling bird who consumed itself by fire then arose from its ashes more splendid and vibrant than before). Just think...You are not a product of myth. You are a *child of God*. Your very inheritance of greatness is founded upon your ability simply...to...believe. And in "believing," there are *major possibilities* that your positive steps toward self-improvement can turn into MASTER PROBABILITIES.

Finally, every time that your faith and self-confidence waver (because they will), I want you to picture the word BELIEVE written vertically in the air just in front of you. Then, recall the follow-

78

ing acrostic and truly absorb what it can mean for you to "believe"—in your vision, your goals…yourself. See and feel the promises that solid belief can hold for your life:

Breaking through

Every cloud…

Leaping over all obstacles…

Imagining and scaling the top of

Each mountain from the

Valley's view…

Embracing awesome probabilities

Also, meditate on these words attributed to the great French painter and sculptor Edgar Degas: "Self-doubt is an insidious enemy; it can kill your talent. Remember never to give in to it!"

If you dare to attack doubt and setbacks with an unconquerable spirit—buoyed by the RIGHT TALK, an undying belief, and a commitment to progressive action—I believe YOU *WILL* FLY!!! Time after time.

Anyone who's going SOMEWHERE follows a plan. Especially those who plan to fly! Now's the time to develop your flight plan. Use the FLIGHT PLAN ESSENTIALS on the next two pages to chart your course to a life filled with the RIGHT TALK.

RIGHT TALK

Flight Plan Essentials

Maintaining a constructive routine is essential to building communication skills. So, commit to developing an improvement plan that includes many (*if not all*) of the following affirmative steps. Use these recommendations to make an INFORMAL CONTRACT with yourself.

Before placing a check in the box in front of a statement you're prepared to commit to, say "I WILL..."

❑ Approach life every day with energy, enthusiasm and a positive attitude.

❑ See myself as a COMMUNICATIONS SUCCESS!

❑ Maintain confident posture.

❑ Maintain a pleasant facial expression.

❑ Focus on ONE THING AT A TIME.

❑ Stay "in the moment"—neither replaying past failure nor rehearsing future disasters.

❑ Make associations between my goals, practice and performance habits and those of top performers and producers around me and on the national scene.

❑ CELEBRATE MYSELF mentally (repeatedly) and aloud (as often as possible).

❑ Display motivational pictures and inspirational sayings at home and at work to keep me "plugged in" to my goal and "charged up" for communications success.

❑ Find at least one communication skills mentor.

❑ Have at least one Super Communicator evaluate my verbal and nonverbal assets & liabilities.

❑ Find a communication skills practice partner.

❑ Look up, learn to pronounce and properly use_____new word(s) each day.

❑ Write each new word, ALL of its definitions and pronunciations in a vocabulary journal—using it in sentences, jotting down any questions for my mentor(s) or a communications expert.

❑ Memorize the meanings of_____prefixes, roots & suffixes each week.

❑ Completely read one book every _____.

❑ Read_____newspaper article(s) daily.

❑ Read_____magazine article(s) weekly.

❑ Watch_____news or information programs weekly.

❑ Use recent-edition reference materials (e.g., a dictionary, thesaurus and glossary) as often as possible.

❑ Use highlighters, red pens & margins to mark memorable reading passages and to write notes, comments or questions.

❑ Keep my language "remodeling" tools (e.g., dictionaries, books, pens & photos) in a prominent place where I can notice and use them daily.

❑ Assemble and travel with a Mobile Communications Mastery Kit (containing my tools & practice sheets and literature about whatever I am working to improve at the time).

❑ Attend a review or refresher English or speech seminar/workshop.

❑ Take a public speaking course.

❑ Attend a motivational session.

❑ Attend inspirational and scripturally-sound church services—regularly.

❑ Develop and practice answers to common interview questions.

❑ Practice "listener-sensitive" telephone skills.

❑ Modulate my tone of voice to be setting- and occasion-appropriate.

❑ Monitor my appearance from head to toe for cleanliness and setting appropriateness.

❑ Have a session with an image consultant.

❑ Trust my instincts when engaged in potentially stressful communication situations (e.g., interviews, business functions, debates, oral presentations, phone calls).

STUDY GUIDE A

CELEBRATE YOURSELF
For Building Self-Esteem

CELEBRATE YOURSELF

1. CELEBRATE YOU! Write a 10-second **self-celebratory statement** (paying special attention to diction and enunciation; you may use *alliteration* OR any other *mnemonic* [memory] *device* to make it catchy or to make it easier to remember).

MNEMONIC DEVICES

ALLITERATION EXAMPLE (The strategic repetition of the "p" sound makes the saying easier to memorize. Choose whatever letter that strikes a chord with you to write your own.)

I am Iris Formey Dawson and I believe God placed me on this planet for the express purpose of inspiring people to aspire to prominent positions by improving their practice and performance in private and public speaking.

ACROSTIC EXAMPLE *A* (Speak of yourself in terms of one of your greatest assets having each leter of the word begin a line of an inspirational poem.)

I am **Iris Formey Dawson** and I am **RESILIENT!**

Remarkably capable of
Emerging from
Stressful
Instances with my
Life
Intact...
Elastic...
Never giving up in
Trying times

ACROSTIC EXAMPLE *B* (Each letter of your name starts a line of a self-affirming poem.)

I am **Iris Formey Dawson** and

I eagerly
Reach for
Inspirational
Stars that

Fill me with
Optimism and
Rich
Motivation to
Explore new territory
Yearly, monthly, weekly and

Daily...
Always
Working to
See golden
Opportunities in both the
Negative and the positive!

2. Memorize what you've written & practice your celebratory statement(s) aloud.

STUDY GUIDE B

ENUNCIATION DRILLS
For Crisper Expression

ENUNCIATION DRILL #1

Practice reading the following words aloud, stressing the frequently swallowed, dropped or slurred sounds in **bold print**.

> **GT KDS** (pronounced "got kids"—to help you remember the often-omitted sounds **g**, **t**, **k**, **d**, **s**)

sen**d**	Carol**'s** house
Jack**'s** kite	writin**g**
plantin**g**	mol**d**
tac**t**	sof**t**
ris**k**	abili**t**y
sof**t**	coul**d** **y**ou
hol**d**	blas**t**
locus**t**	res**t**
han**d**	wha**t** **y**ou
Eric**'s** car	sen**d**
goin**g**	viaduc**t**
connec**t**	promp**t**ly
tol**d**	worl**d**
lef**t**	flas**k**
tes**t**	contrac**t**
tes**ts**	reco**g**nize
shoppin**g**	pas**t**
pac**t**	
pac**k**	
an**d**	
firs**t**	
fol**d**	
lif**t**	
Nia**'s** apple	
respec**t**	

OTHER SOUNDS

get
issue
thing
business
help
I'm
principal
to
figure
with you
Georgia
Virginia
probably
particular
speculation
better
should've
full of
Baptist
sugar
principle
for
four
believe
store
more
manufacture
Joseph ("f" sound)
pamphlet ("f" sound)
potato
calculate
Carolina
participate
government
formulate

ENUNCIATION DRILL #2

Practice reading each of the following tongue twisters, focusing on enunciation.*

Don't ask all acting action heroes to pack an ax; ask if all have awls.

Henry's hens haven't ever had hard hearts or heavy hands.

Pat's pet pit bull pitched a pint of pintos pronto.

Darling Darlene dove for donuts during Dad's different dinner.

Will William will Wild Will forty-four fifties or Twitchy Twila twenty-two twenties?

An elf on a shelf left to himself expects respect even when perturbed by being disturbed.

*NOTE: Be careful to say each word distinctly. Pay special attention to the difference between "ask" and "ax." If you hear no difference, remember that "ask" rhymes with "mask" and "task"…and "ax" rhymes with "max" and "tax."

STUDY GUIDE C

VERB TENSE REFRESHER
For Better Grammar Usage

VERB TENSE REFRESHER*
(See Note 1, p. 95.)

Most verbs, in describing a past (completed) action, simply add -ed to the base (present tense) form of the word, as in *talk, talked* ♦ *finish, finished* ♦ *irrigate, irrigated.* The following lists, however, show verbs that do not follow the regular past tense pattern.** (See Note 2, pp. 95-96.)

1. Note the spelling and pronunciation of each set of verbs.
2. Notice that the *present tense* form (listed in the first column) **adds an -s** to the verb when used with **he, she, it** or **any noun subject**, such as someone or something's name.*** (See Note 3, pp. 96.)
3. Focus on how the *simple past tense* (represented by the middle column) **is NOT formed by adding the regular past tense suffix –ed** to the *base* verb form.
4. Study how the main verb in the *past participial* form (listed in the third column) **may be different from** or **the same as** the verb form listed in one or both of the other columns.

Some *Irregular* Verbs

BASE	PAST	PAST PARTICIPLE
begin [I begin today.] [He/She/It (or a singular noun) begins today.]	began [I began yesterday.] **(recent past action)**	(have, has/had) begun [I **have** begun already.] **(remote past action)**
come	came	(have, has/had) come
drink	drank	(have, has/had) drunk
ring	rang	(have, has/had) rung
run	ran	(have, has/had) run

92

shrink	shr*a*nk	(have, has/had) shr*u*nk
sing	**s*a*ng**	**(have, has/had) s*u*ng**
spring	spr*a*ng	(have, has/had) spr*u*ng
swim	sw*a*m	(have, has/had) sw*u*m

◆◆◆

bet	bet	(have, has/had) bet
burst	burst	(have, has/had) burst
cut	cut	(have, has/had) cut
put	put	(have, has/had) put
set	set	(have, has/had) set

◆◆◆

bring	**brought**	**(have, has/had) brought**
buy	**bought**	**(have, has/had) bought**
catch	caught	(have, has/had) caught
creep	crept	(have, has/had) crept
dig	dug	(have, has/had) dug
fling	flung	(have, has/had) flung
lay	laid	(have, has/had) laid

lend	lent	(have, has/had) lent
lose	lost	(have, has/had) lost
say	said	(have, has/had) said
sit	sat	(have, has/had) sat
sting	stung	(have, has/had) stung
swing	swung	(have, has/had) swung
teach	taught	(have, has/had) taught
think	thought	(have, has/had) thought

◆◆◆

break	**broke**	**(have, has/had) broken**
choose	chose	(have, has/had) chosen
draw	drew	(have, has/had) drawn
drive	**drove**	**(have, has/had) driven**
eat	**ate**	**(have, has/had) eaten**
fall	**fell**	**(have, has/had) fallen**
fly	**flew**	**(have, has/had) flown**

freeze	froze	(have, has/had) frozen
give	**gave**	**(have, has/had) given**
go	**went**	**(have, has/had) gone**
grow	grew	(have, has/had) grown
know	knew	(have, has/had) known
lie	lay	(have, has/had) lain
ride	**rode**	**(have, has/had) ridden**
see	**saw**	**(have, has/had) seen**
shake	**shook**	**(have, has/had) shaken**
speak	spoke	(have, has/had) spoken
steal	stole	(have, has/had) stolen
take	took	(have, has/had) taken
throw	threw	(have, has/had) thrown
write	**wrote**	**(have, has/had) written**

◆◆◆

*To review the definition of "verb" and "noun" refer to the *KEY GRAMMATI-CAL TERMS* sheet at the end of STUDY GUIDE E (p. 111).

Practice and master the use of the **bold print sets first, *paying particular*

95

attention to the verb forms IN THE THIRD COLUMN—which should be used also in the following instances.

(1) With the helping verbs "was" and "were" in the passive voice (when the subject is not performing the action), as in:

SUBJECT

CORRECT: The message was **written** on the envelope.

SUBJECT

INCORRECT: The message was *wrote* on the envelope.

(2) To describe a noun, as in:

CORRECT: The message ***written** on the envelope* was funny.
(The phrase "**written** on the envelope*" describes or tells *which* "message.")

INCORRECT: The message *wrote on the envelope* was funny.
("Wrote" cannot be used to describe. This sentence awkwardly sounds like the *message* did the writing!)

***The verb **be** is COMPLETELY irregular. **UNLIKE ANY OTHER VERB**, it has *three present tense* forms:

I **am**	*NEVER*	I *be*
We, You, They (or plural nouns) **are**	*NEVER*	We, You, They (or "The people/The cars") *be*
He, She, It (or a singular noun) **is**	*NEVER*	He, She, It (or "John/Carol/The car") *be*

And *two simple past tense* forms:

I, He, She, It (or a singular noun) **was**	*NEVER*	I, He, She, It (or "John/Carol/The car") *been*
We, You, They (or plural nouns) **were**	*NEVER*	We, You, They (or "The people/The cars") *been*

[*Been* is not the simple past tense but refers to a time farther in the past. You must use ***has**, **had**,* or ***have*** with *been*.]

96

STUDY GUIDE D

DICTION EXERCISE
For Vocabulary Building

DICTION EXERCISE

The following sentences are examples of simple ways that weak informal expressions and slang creep into our everyday business conversations. Write (in the space below each sentence) a *standard*, more businesslike, word or phrase equivalent for the **underlined/bold print** word or phrase. Then pledge to monitor your speech for other "diction robbers."* (See Note 1, p. 99.)

1. That idea is so **cool**.

2. He purchased a new **ride** for his grandfather.

3. Her philosophy **stinks**.

4. His aunt borrowed his **boom box**.

5. A **chunk** of the plane was recovered yesterday.

6. You shouldn't **slam** your supervisor like that.

7. His father is too uptight; he needs to **chill**.

8. She **blew a gasket** when she heard the news.

9. He **split his side** when he was listening to the new comedian.

10. The model's outfit was **off the chain**, so I bought it immediately.

11. They will **be back in a jiffy**.

12. He **belted** his opponent so hard that his knees buckled.

13. Mr. Madison is a **prune**.

14. Sam is **fixing to** leave us.**

15. He was **shaking in his boots** during the robbery.

16. Before meeting my mentor, I thought studious people were **lame**.

*Consult sources such as *NTC's Dictionary of American Slang and Colloquial Expressions* to determine if words or expressions you commonly use are slang or may be considered inappropriate in some settings.

**"Fixing to" is a chiefly Southern U.S. expression. This example reminds us to be aware of regional differences in language.

STUDY GUIDE E

COMMON PREFIXES, ROOTS/STEMS, AND SUFFIXES
For Vocabulary Building

COMMON PREFIXES, ROOTS/STEMS, AND SUFFIXES

NOTE: If you *really* want to increase your word power, you WILL *STUDY* the lists in this guide (and others like it) **AS OFTEN AS POSSIBLE**. Familiarity with these word parts can improve (1) your reading ability, (2) the quality of your conversations, *and* (3) your verbal test performance.

In some instances, there are references to certain words' *part of speech* (e.g., noun or verb). Should you need to refresh your memory about **the eight parts of speech**, a list appears at the end of this study guide (pp. 111-112).

PREFIXES

WORD PART	MEANING	EXAMPLES
	Greek	
a, an	not	amoral, apathy, anomalous
ambi, amphi	around, both	ambient, amphibious
cata	down	catabolism, catalog, catapult
dia	through	diameter, diaphanous, diarrhea
dys	ill	dysgenic, dyspepsia, dystrophy
ec	out of	eccentric, eclectic, ecstasy
eu	good, well	eulogy, euphoria, evangelize
hyper	over, beyond	hyperbole, hyperglycemic
meta	beyond, change	metamorphosis, metabolic

para	beside	parable, paradigm, parameter
peri	around	perimeter, perinatal, peripheral
syn	with, together	synergy, synthesize, sympathy

Latin

ab	from or away	abdicate, abduct, abstract
ad	to, toward	adapt, addictive, adjure
circum	around	circumflex, circumstance,
com, con	with, together	commerce, conjoined
de	down, away	defer, degrade, depose
dis	apart	dispel, displease, dissident
ex	out, from	excerpt, exclude, expel
extra	beyond	extraneous, extraordinary
inter	between	intercede, interim, interval
intra	within	intranasal, intravenous
non	not	nonessential, nonfiction
ob	against	object, omit, oppress
per	through	perfect, perspire, pervasive
post	after	posthumous, posttraumatic

pro	for, forward, in favor of	proclivity, progress, propel
re	again, back	recriminate, restore, revisit
retro	backward	retroactive, retrograde
se	apart	secede, seclude, secretive
sub	under	subcontract, succumb, supportive
trans	across	transfix, transgress, translate
ultra	beyond, extremely	ultramodern, ultrathin

Anglo-Saxon

a	in, on, at	aboard, abroad, aloft
be	near, by, cause	bedazzle, befriend, beget
for	against, away	forbear, forbid, forswear
fore	before	forecast, foreknow, foretell
mis	wrong, evil	misappropriate, misconstrue
n	not	neither, none, nor
out	beyond	outcast, outdo
over	above, beyond	overcast, overrun, oversell
un	not	unexpected, uninhibited, unearth
under	beneath	undercut, undergo, underwhelm
with	against	withdraw, withhold, withstand

ROOTS

Greek

acr	highest, beginning	acrobat, acronym, acrophobia
auto	self	autograph, autocracy, automate
bibl	book	bibliography, bibliophile
bi, bio	life	biology, bionic, symbiotic
cephal	head	cephalic, encephalitis
chrom	color	chromatophore, monochromatic
chron	time	anachronistic, chronic
demo	the people	demographics, epidemic
derm	skin	dermatitis, taxidermy
gam	to marry	bigamy, exogamic
gnos	knowing	agnostic, diagnosis, prognosis
hetero	different, other	heteronym, heteroplasty
homo	same, common	homologous, homonym
idio	personal, peculiar, private	idiom, idiosyncrasy, idiot
log, logy	to speak, word, study	apology, astrology, logogram
meter, metr	measure	metronome, symmetrical
mis	to hate	misanthrope, misogamy

morph	form, shape	amorphous, metamorphose
neo	new, recent	neogenesis, neophyte
ortho	straight, right	orthochromatic, orthodox
oste	bone	osteopath, osteoporosis
path	feeling, suffering, disease	empathy, pathetic, pathology
polis, polit	city, citizen	cosmopolitan, metropolis
soph	wise	philosopher, unsophisticated
techn	art, skill, craft	architect, technique, technology
theo	god, deity	apotheosis, monotheism

Latin

aequus, aequalis	equal, even	equidistant, inadequacy
audine, auditum	to hear	audible, audience, auditory
bene	good, well	benediction, benevolent
caput, capitis	head	capital, captain, decapitate
cedere, cessum	to go, move along	concede, procession, recede
dicere, dictum	to say, tell, speak	dictate, malediction, verdict
ducere, ductum	to lead	aqueduct, deduce, ductile
facere, factum	to do, make	effect, factitious, factory

106

fallere, falsum	to deceive	fallacious, falsify, infallible
gradi, gressum	to step, go	digress, graduation, ingredient
grex, gregis	herd, flock	aggregate, congregate, segregate
haerere, haesum	to stick, cling	adhesive, coherent, heretic
ire, itineris, itum	to go, a journey	circuit, exit, itinerary
jungere, junctum	to join	adjunct, conjuncture, junction
jus, juris	right, justice	injurious, jurisdiction, jury
laborare	to work	collaborate, laboratum, elaborate, laborious
lingua	tongue, language	linguistic, lingulate, sublingual
malus, malignus	bad, of evil nature	maladaptive, malfeasance
mater, matris	mother	maternal, matriarch, matrix
negare, negatum	to say no	negation, renegade, renege
novus	new	novelty, novice, renovate
oculus	eye	binocular, monocle, ocular
os, ossis	bone	ossification, osteitis
pax, pacis	peace	appeasement, pacifism, pay
par, paris	equal	disparity, paripinnate
quaerere, quaesitum	to seek for, ask	query, quest, require
rudis	rough, undeveloped	rude, rudimentary

rumpere, ruptum	to break, burst	disrupt, eruptive, rupture
sacer, sacrum	holy, sacred	desecrate, sacrilege, sacrarium
scribere, scriptum	to write	prescribe, proscribe, scribe
trahere, tractum	to draw, pull	attractive, subtract, traction
tempus, temporis	time	extemporaneous, temporal
uti, usus, sum	to use, employ	abuse, usury, utile
venire, ventum	to come	preventative, revenue, venture
verus	true	aver, veracity, verification

SUFFIXES

Anglo-Saxon

ar	**liar** - *one who* lies
ard	**drunkard** - *one who* drinks
ation	**creation** - *process of* creating; **flirtation** - *action of* flirting; **liberation** - *the state, condition* or *quality of*
dom	**kingdom** - *state of* a king; **stardom** - *condition of* being a star
en	**earthen** - *made of* earth; **golden** - *like* or *suggestive of* gold
en	*form verbs from adjectives* [cheap, **cheapen**] *and nouns* [strength, **strengthen**]
er	**dreamer** - *one who* dreams; **swimmer** - *one who* swims
ern	**western** - *relating to* the west
ful	**masterful** - *resembling* a master; **mouthful** - *a quantity that fills* the mouth; **playful** - *full of* play; **useful** - *able to* use
hood	**fatherhood** - *state of being* a father; **sisterhood** - *a group sharing the qualities of* sisters
ie	**doggie** - a *little* dog; **townie** - *one having to do with* a town

ion	**completion** - *process of* completing; **dehydration** - *state or condition of being* dehydrated
ish	**brownish** - *somewhat* brown; **girlish** - *having the characteristics of* a girl
kin	**lambkin** - a *little* lamb
let	**ringlet** - a *little* ring; **starlet** - a *little* star
like	**ladylike** - *like* a lady; **lifelike** - *like* real life
ling	**duckling** - a *little* duck; **shearling** - a *young* sheared sheep
ly	**manly** - *lik*e a man; **sisterly** - *resembling* a sister
ly	**weekly** - *at a specified interval of time* (a week); **hourly** - *recurring at a specified interval of time* (an hour)
ly	**slowly** - *in a* slow *way*; **smartly** - *in a* smart *manner*
ness	**brightness** - *quality* or *condition of being* bright; **sadness** - *state of being* sad
ock	**hillock** - a *little* hill; **paddock** - a *piece of* fenced in land
ship	**kingship** - *condition of being* a king
ship	**professorship** - *rank, status,* or *office of being* a professor
ship	**penmanship** - *art, skill,* or *craft of* handwriting
ship	**readership** - *a collective body of* readers
some	**bothersome** - *characterized by* bother; **worrisome** - *tending to* worry
some	**threesome** - *a group of* three
ster	**roadster** - a horse *used for* the road; **songster** - *one who makes* songs; **youngster** - *one who is* young
tude	**fortitude** - *quality of* strength; **servitude** - *condition, state,* or *quality of being* forced to labor for free
ty	**faulty** - *condition, state,* or *quality of having* a fault; **gravity** - *condition, state,* or *quality of being* grave or serious
ty	**forty** - four *times ten*
ward	**eastward** - *in the direction of* the east; **skyward** - *toward* the sky
y	**clayey** - *consisting of* clay; **summery** - *like* summer
y	**sleepy** - *tending toward* sleep
y	**jealousy** - *condition, state,* or *quality of being* jealous

y	**lumpy** - *covered or filled with* lumps; **steamy** - *having the qualities of* or *full of* steam
yer	**lawyer** - *one who* practices law; **sawyer** - *one who* saws

Latin

able	**doable** - *able to be* done; **refundable** - *able to* refund
an	**librarian** - *one who* works in a library; **partisan** - *one who* takes part
an	**American** - *related to* America; **Spartan** - *related to* a strict, rigid style
ance	**reassurance** - *act of* reassuring; **reliance** - *act of* relying
ancy	**buoyancy** - *quality of* lightness; **pregnancy** - *condition of* being pregnant
ant	**miscreant** - *one who* does or believes badly; **sycophant** - *one who* seeks favor through flattery
ar	**polar** - *of, relating to,* or *referring to* a pole; **solar** - *of, relating to,* or *referring to* the sun
ar	**angular** - *like* an angle; **stellar** - *like* a star
ble	**debatable** - *worthy of* being debated; **reliable** - *able to be* relied upon
ee	**assignee** - *one who is* assigned as an agent; **devotee** - *one who is* devoted
ent	**referent** - *one that* refers; **student** - *one who* studies
ent	**ambivalent** - *being* uncertain; **salient** - *being* prominent or conspicuous
eer	**auctioneer** - *one who* holds an auction; **balladeer** - *one who* sings ballads
ible	**corrigible** - *able to be* corrected; **susceptible** - *able to be* influenced or affected
ic	**acidic** - *like* acid; **caloric** - *of* or *relating to* calories
ify	**calcify** - *to make or become* stony or inflexible; **rectify** - *to make* right
ine	**bovine** - *of* or *relating to* a cow; **equine** - *of* or *relating to* a horse

ment **settlement** - *that which is* settled
ment **retirement** - *state of being* retired
ment **appeasement** - *the act of* appeasing
mony **acrimony** - *that which is* sharp or harsh
mony **matrimony** - *condition of being* married;
      harmony - *state of being* in agreement
or   **benefactor** - *one who* gives aid; **accelerator** - *one that* accelerates
or   **rancor** - *state of* deep resentment; **valor** - *quality of* bravery
ose   **morose** - *abounding in* gloom; **bellicose** - *abounding in* ill temper
ous   **joyous** - *full of* joy; **viscous** - *having much* resistance to flow
ulent **turbulent** - *full of* agitation; **virulent** - *abounding in* infection or poison
ure   **disclosure** - *act of* disclosing; **licensure** - *act of* licensing
ure   **legislature** - *that which* legislates; **erasure** - *that which is* erased

KEY GRAMMATICAL TERMS

The Eight Parts of Speech

NOUN	names a person, place, thing, idea, or quality
PRONOUN	takes the place of a noun
VERB	shows action or states a condition
ADJECTIVE	describes a noun or pronoun (tells *how much, how many, what kind, which one*)
ADVERB	modifies a verb, an adjective, or another adverb (describes *how, how much, when* and *where*)
PREPOSITION	joins a noun or pronoun to the rest of the sentence; shows place in space *or* position in time

111

CONJUNCTION connects words, phrases, *or* clauses

INTERJECTION shows strong feeling *or* expresses sudden emotion

The Parts of a Sentence*

SUBJECT noun, pronoun *or* phrase used as a noun that tells *whom* or *what* the sentence is about OR *who* or *what* performs the action

PREDICATE a verb and the word(s) used to explain the action or condition

OBJECT receives the action of a verb OR is a noun or pronoun related to the rest of the sentence by a preposition

PHRASE a group of closely-related words, having no subject or predicate (may function as an adjective, adverb, noun or verb)

CLAUSE a group of words having a subject and a predicate (An independent or main clause can stand alone as a complete sentence. A dependent or subordinate clause is incomplete by itself.)

*To be considered complete, every sentence must have *a subject* and *a predicate*. However, occasionally in some styles of writing, either the subject or the predicate of a sentence may be omitted when it can be readily understood from preceding or following sentences. Naturally, in both formal and informal speaking situations, this practice occurs even more frequently.

STUDY GUIDE F

CONVERSATION STARTERS
For Heightening Verbal Charm

CONVERSATION STARTERS

Use this list to prepare for *initiating conversation* and *responding* (if engaged in a discussion about any of the listed topics). Practice talking about a few of these each day.

1. Introduce/Reintroduce yourself to someone; then ask him/ her: "What's the most rewarding community activity you're involved in?"

2. Ask someone to tell you about a hobby or special interest he/she has.

3. Discuss a current event.

4. Ask someone what he/she does for a living, for how long, and why & how he/she got started. If the person is a domestic engineer, ask him/her for home management tips.

5. Ask someone if he/she has children. If so, ask him/her to tell you about the child or children.

6. Discuss a recent event you attended or watched on television (theater, sports, concert).

7. Discuss a good book you've recently heard of, read, or plan to read.

8. Ask someone to share three interesting/exciting things about himself/herself. Tell him/her three interesting/ exciting things about yourself.

9. Ask someone: "How do you relax?" Then, tell what you like to do.

10. Ask someone: "If you could change professions, what would you do?"

11. Ask someone: "If you could live in any other city or town tomorrow, where would you live?"

12. Ask someone: "Do you know of a really good florist in town?"

13. Ask someone: "What would you do if you woke up tomorrow and had no means to support yourself?"

14. Give someone directions from your home to the county courthouse.

15. Tell someone your opinion of the local public school system and why you feel as you do.

16. Ask someone to tell you about his/her dream car. Ask about why it appeals to him/her.

17. Tell someone about an unusual or special skill of yours.

18. Tell someone about an excellent place to volunteer in town.

19. Tell someone about a great historic site you have visited.

20. Ask someone to give you gift ideas for a specific hard-to-shop-for relative.

21. Discuss your opinion of home schooling.

22. Tell someone the wisest thing anyone has ever told you.

23. Ask someone to share the best career networking tips he/ she has ever heard.

24. Describe your mother or father in one word. Explain why you chose that word.

25. Tell someone about your greatest obstacle in life and what you did (or are doing) to overcome it.

26. Tell someone about a time you made a mistake.

27. Ask someone to share his/her most impressive trait.

28. Tell someone about a time you handled a difficult situation well.

29. Ask someone what he/she believes was the most significant invention of the 20th Century.

30. Disclose your greatest weakness to someone. Tell what you are doing to keep that deficiency from becoming a permanent liability.

FREQUENTLY-ASKED INTERVIEW QUESTIONS

The structure and content of interviews, along with the type and number of questions asked, may vary greatly from one organization to the next and from one interviewer to another. Also, the sort and level of position may affect the depth and often the manner of questioning. While entry-level interviews may last only a few minutes, more advanced interviews may require a few extended rounds. Thus, there is no ONE way to prepare properly for an interview.

So, here—from the simple to the complex—is a list of 20 common interview questions to get you started. Practice handling them alone *and* with mock interviewers. For actual interviews, be sure to tailor your responses to fit the position and culture of the company in which you are interested.

1. Tell me about yourself.

2. What keywords would your peers use to describe you?

3. What are your greatest strengths?

4. Describe your greatest weaknesses and tell what you've done to overcome them.

5. Why should we hire you?

6. What can you contribute to our organization?

7. In analyzing a problem, what steps do you take?

8. Where do you see your career five years from now?

9. What sets you apart from other applicants for this position?

10. How do you maintain an effective working relationship with your coworkers?

11. How well do you work independently?

12. What are the chief characteristics of a good team member?

13. The ideal work team would consist of what types of people?

14. Tell about a situation you were in that would demonstrate your ability to work under pressure.

15. Briefly describe the most significant responsibility you have had and what it taught you.

16. Describe a situation in which your work was criticized; then tell how you responded to that criticism.

17. What can a supervisor do to strengthen teamwork in an organization?

18. Tell about a time when you came up with a creative solution to a problem.

19. Your expenditures for office supplies have increased by 50% over the past two years.

    What steps will you take to control and reduce expenditures?

20. How do you manage on-the-job risk?

STUDY GUIDE G

ORAL PRESENTATION TIPS
For Adding Icing to the Communications Cake

ORAL PRESENTATION TIPS

Solid presentations are built on excellence in the following foundational areas:

- **Audience/Occasion/Purpose Appropriateness** (In organizing *and* delivery, take into consideration your audience members' backgrounds—e.g., age, gender, profession/job position, educational level. You may need to adjust your presentations accordingly. Be sure that your remarks or discussion fit the occasion, setting, and purpose for which you are speaking.)

- **Originality** (Who wants to hear "the same old thing" said "the same old way"? Refresh your audiences by allowing them to see, hear and feel YOU. Defy convention; give a new twist to an old theme/topic. Speak *memorably* or DON'T SPEAK AT ALL.)

- **Organization/Coherence** (For smooth flow, arrange your thoughts logically, being sure to present points coherently. Take time [1] to compose a *riveting*, "orienting" opening; [2] to include smooth, clear transitions; and [3] to develop a solid, thought- or action-provoking conclusion. Also, get your materials together WELL IN ADVANCE.)

- **Appearance** (Look "large and in charge." Beforehand, pay attention to even the smallest details of your hygiene, dress and grooming. During your presentation, monitor your facial expression and posture.)

- **Poise** (Coolness, composure, ease, naturalness, self-possession in delivery and handling distractions can "make" your performance. On the other hand, excessive use of *filler words* and *phrases* [e.g., "uh," "um," "like" & "you know"] and *verbal tics* [e.g., breathiness, throat clearing, smacking & snorting] can weaken your appeal. Also, your poise index skyrockets when you can deal smoothly with embarrassing, startling or potentially upsetting situations (e.g., tripping or falling, equipment malfunction, or heckling).

- **Voice Projection/Volume** (Manage your volume appropriately for your room size, audience & effect—use a microphone if necessary. Remember that, in some instances, strategically raising or lowering your voice can have a powerful impact. It can emphasize a point beautifully.)

- **Tone** (Showing appropriate animation/obvious passion for your topic [1] reflects *on* your sincerity and commitment and [2] is reflected *by* not only your voice but also your preparedness, the backdrop established & your appearance. Your tone can *turn on* an audience or cause them to *tune out*.)

- **Pitch** (*Deep breathing* [using the lower abdominal muscles] produces a richer, warmer sound; whereas, *shallow breathing* [using the throat] produces a higher, tenser sound.)

- **Diction** (Choose and use words EFFECTIVELY. Throughout, be sure to use precise, evocative [image-creating] language that best serves both your theme and your audience.)

- **Pronunciation** (Nail down potential problem words/names— LONG BEFORE you begin. If need be, consult a dictionary and/or knowledgeable individuals.)

- **Enunciation** (Crispness counts—Don't swallow your middle sounds or leave off endings, e.g., G, O, T, K, D, S, A, R, E)

- **Rate** (Go neither too fast nor too slow; instead, vary your pace to fit the audience and specific points. Do not let pauses interfere with the flow of your presentation.)

- **Eye Contact** (With small groups, be sure to connect with the eyes of every audience member—*at least once.* For larger groups, direct visual attention to all sections (front, back, center, left & right.)

- **Movement** (Unless restricted to a lectern, be comfortable with it as a "home base;" don't "grow roots" there! *Work the room or platform* [walk around—but don't pace]. Use appropriate, message-enhancing, natural gestures/body language. Don't fidget with hair, clothes, pens, etc. Handle notes and visuals with ease.)

- **Time** (Speak *for the time allotted.* Never go over without the permission of your host and/or the audience. Also, try not to end much earlier than expected.)

Sharpening these elements is *key* to establishing and maintaining both a command over your material *and* a positive relationship with your audience. You cannot afford simply to choose the ones you will *try* to do well. Missing the mark on *any* of them could sabotage your message. But mastering them ALL...could send you *and* your audience SOARING!

Resources

Carson, Ben. *Think Big: Unleashing Your Potential for Excellence*. Grand Rapids, MI: Zondervan Publishing House, 1996.

Fry, Edward Bernard. *The Reading Teacher's Book of Lists*. Englewood Cliffs, NJ: Prentice Hall, 1993.

Gill, N.S. *"A Little Etymology: If You Recognize the Parts, You'll Understand the Whole," Ancient/Classical History Guide*. About.com, 2002.

Hayford, Jack W., ed. *Spirit-Filled Life Bible*. Nashville: Thomas Nelson Publishers, 1991.

Jeffers, Susan J. *Feel the Fear and Do It Anyway*. New York: Fawcett Book Group, 1996.

Job-Interview.net. *Job Interview Questions and Answers*. PSC Network, 2001.

Lucado, Max. *Let the Journey Begin: God's Roadmap for New Beginnings*. Nashville: J. Countryman, 1999.

Mayer, Lyle V. *Fundamentals of Voice and Articulation*. New York: McGraw-Hill Higher Education, 1998.

Mayer, Lyle V. *Fundamentals of Voice and Diction*. New York: Brown and Benchmark, 1993.

McKay, Matthew. *Messages: The Communication Skills Book*. Oakland, CA: New Harbinger Publications, 1995.

Moore, Bob & Maxine Moore, eds. *Dictionary of Latin and Greek Origins*. Lincolnwood, IL: NTC Publishing Group, 2000.

Peale, Norman Vincent. *The Power of Positive Thinking*. New York: Fawcett Book Group, 1976.

Pinker, Steven. *Words and Rules: The Ingredients of Language.* New York: HarperTrade, 2000.

Sabin, William A. *The Gregg Reference Manual*, Ninth Edition. New York: Glencoe/McGraw-Hill, 2000.

Seitz, Victoria A. *Your Executive Image: How to Look Your Best and Project Success for Men and Women.* Avon, MA: Adams Media Corporation, 2000.

Shertzer, Margaret. *The Elements of Grammar.* New York: Macmillan Publishing Company, 1986.

Spears, Richard A. *NTC's Dictionary of American Slang and Colloquial Expressions.* New York: McGraw-Hill/Contemporary, 2000.

The American Heritage Dictionary of the English Language, Fourth Edition. Boston, MA: Houghton Mifflin Company, 2000.

Yate, Martin J. *Knock 'Em Dead 2002: The Ultimate Job Seeker's Resource with Great Answers to over 200 Tough Interview Questions.* Avon, MA: Adams Media Corporation, 2001.

ABOUT
ARTISON ASSOCIATES

Training...Outside the Box SM

Artison Associates is a Savannah, Georgia-based performance improvement consultancy. The company specializes in customizing seminars, workshops, motivational presentations and coaching sessions to meet the specific needs of corporate, community, and individual clients. *We deliver dynamic, informative, innovative & inspirational* sessions that can change the way you, your team members, clients or students approach life and "get the job done"...

With us, tailoring our presentations to the distinctive makeup of each client is always a priority. Whether we're coaching an individual or redirecting a whole organization, we prove that effective training *can be exciting*—in just about any area—at just about any time—for clients of all ages. Working with you to meet your needs, we design and deliver UNFORGETTABLE multi-sensory, interactive experiences that leave lasting positive impressions!

PRINCIPAL SEMINARS & WORKSHOPS

Building Interpersonal Relations Skills

Key topics...
- Analyzing Self
- Understanding & Adapting to Personality Types
- Developing & Maintaining Trust
- Managing Anger
- Listening Effectively
- Sending Effective Professional Messages
- Processing Feedback
- Analyzing Sexual Harassment Issues
- Resolving Conflicts
- Relation"ship" Building

Cultural Diversity

Key topics...
- Benefits of a Multicultural Vision
- 10 Key Dimensions of Diversity
- Equity *vs.* Equality
- Service Delivery in a Diverse Setting
- T.I.P.S. for Facilitating Culturally-Competent Interaction

Light-Year Leadership™

Key topics...
- Self-Definition
- Success Assessment
- Goal-Setting & Attainment
- Critical Issues in Management
- Team Building
- Customer Service Excellence

Managing Stress

Key topics...
- Negative Stimulants
- Common Trouble Spots
- Two Major Dimensions of Stress
- Personal and Interpersonal Stress Management
- Communication Skills
- Empathy Development
- "Bridging" Strategies

Polishing Professionalism

Key topics...
- The 7-Second Assessment
- Self-image *vs.* Reputation
- The Dimensions of Professional Appearance—At Work & Away
- Interpersonal Relations
- Peak Professional Performance

Right Talk™

Key topics...
- Common Trouble Spots • Physical Image
- Pronunciation Mastery • Body Language
- Enunciation • Business Social Mixing
- Diction • Interview Techniques
- Vocabulary Building • Business Presentations
- Public Speaking • Telephone Skills

Executive Communications Coaching*

Key features...
- Needs Assessment • Communications Assets & Liabilities Profile
- Customized Development Plan • Study Guide
- Weekly Consultations • Quick-Call Grammar & Phrasing Assistance
- Weekly Professional Development E-Newsletter • Development Review
- Maintenance Plan Development

Topflight Heights™

Key topics...
- Common Counterproductive Patterns
- Exploring "Self"
- The Dynamics of Diversity
- The Nature of a Strong Team
- Concentrated Communications
- Achieving Balance
- Problem-Solving Strategies

*A confidential speech & writing enhancement service customized in consideration of clients' privacy and time constraints.

Verve Serve™

Key topics...
- The High Price of Poor Service
- The Big Payoffs of Premium Service
- The Cornerstones of Customer Service
- Image Makers & Image Breakers
- Essential Elements of Change
- Managing Complaints
- Innovative Campaigns

Writing Rescue™

Key topics...
- Pre-Writing Steps
- Conquering Writer's Block
- Common Grammar Problems
- Sentence & Paragraph Development
- Developing Style
- Proofreading & Editing

We also customize motivational sessions and keynote addresses according to your <u>adult or youth</u> event theme!

For a list of our most popular presentations, check out
www.ArtisonAssociates.com.

To arrange a session, call **912-920-3899**
or submit a request at our website.

About Artison Publications

Artison Publications is an imprint of **ARTISON ASSOCIATES**. Established in 1999, for the express purpose of packaging and distributing the company's instructional and inspirational resources, **Artison Publications** produces novelty communications items, audio and video recordings as well as print materials.

OTHER ARTISON PRODUCTS

RIGHT TALK ™: *A Pathway to Greater Personal and Family Success*
(videocassette tape)

Like the participants in this dynamic seminar, you will be inspired and enlightened as Iris unfolds how individuals and families can use Artison's distinctive **Quad *E* to Excellence Principle** to STRENGTHEN PERSONAL AND "FAMILY TEAM" COMMUNICATION SYSTEMS.

SOUR NOTES ™
(audiocassette tape/CD with companion study guide *or* videocassette tape with workbook)

Using Iris's creative step-by-step approach, *in one hour* you can LEARN *HOW* TO PRONOUNCE **EVERY WORD** IN THE ENGLISH LANGUAGE—then become proficient at using the system in as little as two weeks!

RULE TOOLS ™
(videocassette tape with companion study guide)

In this GRAMMAR REVIEW, Iris's innovative and upbeat teaching style will easily refresh your grasp of key rules (e.g., verb tenses, subject-verb agreement, pronoun usage).

ANIMATE LAMINATES ™
(motivational book marks and wallet cards)

Everyday TERMS AND PHRASES COME ALIVE to remind you to look at many of life's common issues from a fresh perspective. Choose from a wide variety (e.g., *"Greatness," "Family," "Team Building," "Diversity"* & *"Reach"*).

FRAMEABLE NAMES ™
(inspirational onomastic sayings—framed and matted)

Poems built from *your name* or *any other*—these ACROSTICS keep you or someone else special inspired about personal greatness by showing you just "what's in a name!"

MUFFIE LOU AND THE SPECIAL GIFT
(*children's picture book + companion song on audiocassette*)

Preschoolers through 2nd-graders will delight in discovering the special gift of "courtesy" as they learn *what to say* and *what to do* and *how to sing* Muffie Lou's signature song, *"Be Polite."*

MUFFIE LOU AND THE BARBECUE
(*children's picture book + companion song on audiocassette*)

A fun story for preschoolers through 2nd-graders to explore the family values of "caring & sharing." Features another Muffie Lou musical favorite.

To order these products or additional copies of this book, call **912-920-3899** or submit a request at **www.ArtisonAssociates.com.**

HENDERSON E. FORMEY, JR. passed away January 17, 2002. In support of his mission to facilitate others' self-improvement and higher education, his family has established a memorial fund. Enriched by the same public school system he helped fortify, each of Formey's seven children earned academic scholarships to some of America's most prestigious institutions of higher learning: Carleton, Williams, Connecticut, and Macalester colleges and Princeton and Yale universities.

◆◆◆

To assist the family in our efforts to share the gifts of exposure and experience our parents afforded us, you may send a donation to:

THE HENDERSON E. FORMEY FUND FOR SCHOLARS
c/o SunTrust Bank, Savannah
P.O. Box 8668
Savannah, GA 31412-8668

THANK YOU FOR YOUR SUPPORT.